# The Backpacking with Kids Handbook

## Your down and dirty guide to fun outdoor adventures with your kids

### *Kenda Alexander*

Mt. Hood from Bald Mountain
Photo courtesy of Christopher Skipper © 2016

©2017 Kenda Alexander
All rights reserved. This book or parts thereof may not be reproduced in any form, stored in any retrieval system, or transmitted in any form by any means—electronic, mechanical, photocopy, recording, or otherwise—without prior written permission of the publisher, except as provided by the United States of America copyright law. For permission requests, write to the publisher, at "Attention: Permissions Coordinator," at the address below.

Kenda Alexander
P.O. Box 851
Welches, OR  97067

www.kendaalexander.com

kendaalexanderauthor@google.com

## Table of Contents

**Chapter 1: Why I Backpack With My Kids**
**Chapter 2: Jungle Gyms and Trail Monkeys**
    Getting fit for backpacking
**Chapter 3: Slow and Steady**
    Realistic expectations for hiking with kids
**Chapter 4: Just Keep Swimming**
    How to keep kids moving up the trail while making it fun for everyone
**Chapter 5: Wildflowers and Zoology**
    Trips with a special focus
**Chapter 6: Soup, Nuts, and the Kitchen Sink**
    Well-fed kids are happy hikers
**Chapter 7: The Monkey on Your Back**
    5 steps for reducing pack weight
**Chapter 8: Don't Wear Cotton!**
    Clothing and footwear for the trail
**Chapter 9: At Home in the Wilderness**
    How to set up camp and get kids involved
**Chapter 10: Always Something to Do**
    What to do in camp when kids get bored
**Chapter 11: Perfect Potty Solutions**
    How to take kids potty in the outdoors
**Chapter 12: Choose Your View**
    How to determine a kid friendly hike
**Chapter 13: Here and Back Again**
    How not to get lost in the woods

**Chapter 14: Put This in Your Pack**
        The gear you need and nothing more

**Chapter 15: Bears Live Here**
        How to keep kids safe in the wild


**Appendix A: Safety Kits and Skills**
        How to build kid friendly safety kits

# Chapter 1
# Why I Backpack With My Kids

"Momma, Momma ... just stop and admire it!"

How can I refuse? I stop and admire the tiny waterfall shooting out over the trail and soak in the beauty my 11-year-old son points out. He sees my beloved wilderness with fresh eyes. I enjoy the little waterfall in a completely new way while hiking with him.

The long spring rains have finally stopped and we are taking advantage of every minute to get out and enjoy some long overdue sunshine. Today, it's a hike on our favorite local trail. This is one of our "backyard" hikes. It's only a 10 minute drive from home and easy to access most of the year.

All the tiny streams are rushing with water this early in the spring. We skirt around the waterfall and continue east. The sun sparkles off the swift running Salmon River inviting a toe dip– which quickly reminds us it's still early spring in the mountains! But the sun is warm and the day is bright and we enjoy every minute of our hike along the spongy trail.

There are multiple stream crossings and soggy parts of the trail to navigate, but the lower 2 mile portion of the trail is snow free nearly year round. My kids are spread out on the trail ahead of me. They know every inch of these familiar woods. My teens are deep into a challenge to see who can reach the viewpoint, 4 miles ahead, first.

The trail travels through a forest of giant Western and Mountain hemlock, Douglas fir and Western red cedar trees mixed with Red alder and Vine maple. Patches of leftover winter snow hide in the shadows where shoots of Devil's Club and Baneberry poke through, warning us where the swampy places will be as the snow melts. Snowbells and trilliums blossom on the forest floor beside tart wood sorrel. I know my kids have been feasting on the little 4-leaf plants. Soon False Solomon's Seal and Bleeding Hearts will be blooming and fragrant on the sunny south facing slopes.

In the summer we hike to our favorite swimming hole less than a ½ mile from the trailhead. Here the trail is cut into a rocky cliff face that swoops down into the depths of the river. The river bends and creates a perfect eddy, deep and calm enough for swimming. If you can stand the cold! The river is fed by many small streams and springs on its 33.5 mile journey from the base of Palmer Glacier high on Mt. Hood to its confluence at the Sandy River and remains joint-aching cold year round. Still, we come when the days are hot and we can warm ourselves on the rocks. And while the water is cold for us, it is a comfortable home for baby Chinook salmon left to grow, swim to the ocean, then return to spawn just as their parents did. Like the salmon, steelhead conquer the hundreds of mile journey from the ocean back to these crystalline waters to begin the cycle over again. Cutthroat and rainbow trout thrive in the cold water and hide in the pools and riffles all year long.

In the fall we stand on the trail high above the clear river and spot the body of a dead salmon lying on the bottom, offering its spent body as food to tiny invertebrates. These are then fed on by baby salmon and trout. Crawdads thrive on the feast and Steller's Jays and crows grow fat and sleek on the rotting debris while keeping the shore clean. Even bears, foxes and coyotes take advantage of dead salmon lying along the edges of the river, readying themselves for the winter months ahead with this rich source of fat and protein. Nothing goes to waste in the wild. Just off the trail on the leaf littered forest floor, we hunt for delicious yellow chanterelle mushrooms for our winter feasts.

My two youngest run back and forth along the trail, checking in, exuberantly sharing discoveries they've made. Our family dog runs with them, tongue hanging from the side of his smiling doggy mouth. Hiking is good. After about 3 hours we chug up the last mile, climbing to the viewpoint. The two youngest are with me now and I can't help giving them a motherly reminder to stay away from the edge. They already know. I hook the leash onto the collar of our dog just to be safe. My three teens are already at the viewpoint, digging into lunches they've carried in their daypacks. We join them, glad for the rest in the warm spring sun.

If you look carefully, you can see Frustration Falls far below where the Salmon River flows through the narrow gorge. The kids point it out to each other. Meanwhile, I'm making plans.

"Do you guys want to do a weekend trip to Burnt Lake next month?"

"Will there be lots of snow like last time?" queries my oldest. She's referring to a trip we took when she was much younger. It was a high snowfall year. We never did make it to the lake that day.

"Shouldn't be, things are melting off early."

"Sure. But everyone has to help carry stuff." She knows the drill and expects her younger siblings to help out.

"Of course"

And we plan, there on the rocky point overlooking the deep Salmon River gorge, surrounded by tiny spring wildflowers blooming in the warm sun. I already anticipate the fun we'll have. I imagine the beauty we'll see and I'm excited about the adventure we'll experience.

I love backpacking in all its forms: solo trips, where I can soak up the silence, trips with my husband, where time in camp is so simple and relaxed, long trips with friends, full of accomplishment and new sights. We cover lots of ground and laugh ourselves gut sore. But backpacking trips with my kids have been the most rewarding of all. Admittedly, they have been the most work. All those years of teaching them and investing in them took patience. But the returns on our investments have been amazing. Far greater than I expected. I don't regret a single moment of the effort. The memories of fatigue from carrying extra gear or a tired toddler just make time on the trail with competent teens and young adults that much sweeter. Watching them move around camp setting up tarps, building fires, and cooking meals is heavenly. And a bit of payback while I sit and relax.

I started backpacking with my kids when they were in the womb. Each of them has been carried in a front pack on many trips. Even when backpacking got tricky with 5 kids under 9, we still found a way to get out into the wilds, if only for day hikes and car camping trips.

Backpacking has many elements to consider and it can feel intimidating to try and figure it all out with kids in tow. I believe it's possible for anyone to learn the basics as they explore their neighborhoods and nearby trails.

I was already an experienced backpacker when I started having kids so my learning curve was somewhat less steep than for someone just starting out. But we still had to ease into it. I didn't know how to manage diapers on the trail at first. I was worried about my babies sleeping warm enough in a tent. We learned by trial and error how to keep our kids moving up the trail in spite of being tired. I overloaded my first born on a few trips before realizing it wasn't fun for her anymore. We made mistakes and had a few less than ideal nights in the woods. Not once were we in danger and every situation taught us how to do it better next time.

We took lots of walks in our neighborhood and explored our local park to build up our endurance and test out gear. I discovered many valuable things on these short trips. We learned that ill-fitting footwear is agony for everyone, even little walkers. We found raingear that shredded at the first breath of breeze and raingear that actually worked to keep everyone dry. We found out which child carriers were comfortable and which were not. These little day trips were gold in preparing us for our first overnighters and weekend campouts.

After the birth of each child, we had to make adjustments. We had to shorten our trips until little legs grew longer. We had to explore lighter gear so we could somehow carry all we needed for 4, then 5, then 6, then 7 people. We started out like most people, using freeze dried backpacking food from our local outdoor store. It didn't settle too well on our stomachs and was more expensive than it was worth. So we scoured our grocery store to see what might be easy to cook on the trail. There were instant soups and noodle cups. Cheap and light but not very filling as kids grew. We ate boxes and boxes of instant oatmeal, though I never liked the sugar in most of them. But even these cheap grocery store finds got expensive. So we started experimenting at home with drying our own food, making our own oatmeal mixes, and making jerky. We liked the better flavors and more comfortable digestion. We liked getting to choose our meals instead of being at the mercy of what our grocery store carried. I checked out every book in our local library on dehydrating food, backpacking food, and storing food–multiple times. That was before the amazing internet that puts all that research right in your lap.

I became a catalogue hoarder for a time. Spending the winter months searching for clothes and gear that would make all this easier. And that we could afford. Most trips when the kids were young did not include top of the line gear. We wore cotton (gasp!) and took plenty of backups to make sure everyone had dry clothes to wear. We used what we had and it worked out just fine. Step by step we learned and we kept taking walks and going on day hikes and taking backpacking trips. It didn't happen overnight but the journey was just as valuable as the experience we can claim now.

All 5 of my kids survived our backpacking adventures and each one has an appreciation for the wilderness that comes from experiencing it up close. Some of them love backpacking more than others now, but all of them learned valuable skills and each one has the confidence that they can manage all their needs in the wilds.

It is my hope that this book will help you take your first steps into the wilderness with your kids. If you are already a seasoned backpacker, you'll make the transition to taking your kids along easily. If you are new to backpacking, you will learn right along with your kids. However tentative or bold your first steps are, you will get there. You will savor the moments of discovery right along with the hard work and patience. I promise you won't regret one minute of the time and energy you invest.

## Chapter 2
# Jungle Gyms and Trail Monkeys
### Getting fit for backpacking

**Tips**
- play outdoors
- let your kids go barefoot
- model a love of the outdoors
- take lots of day hikes
- develop a lifestyle of active outdoor living

Cool mist from Ramona Falls beads droplets on our faces. We're standing on the wooden bridge just below the cascade. It feels good after the nearly 4 mile hike on the dusty trail. We enjoy the view of the deeply shaded falls. Sunlight filters through the trees making the misty waters glow where touched by light. The crystal water falls from 120 feet above us, splashing down the stair step basalt rock face. Our girls are just past toddler stage. They both hiked most of the trip and are dirty from head to toe. They are anxious to play in the creek below the falls so we take them below the bridge to splash around in the pools.

Finally, the dust is washed off and they get tired of playing in the water. We dry them off with a cheap "dusting" towel I bought from a dollar store. We put the extra t-shirts on and have a snack before heading down the trail back to the car. I know the clean t-shirts will be a dusty mess by the time we get there.

The trail back follows Ramona creek downstream for about a mile. We stop and toss sticks into the creek and then race down to see them fall over miniature waterfalls. Then the trail leaves the creek side and becomes a sandy footpath once more. We're pleasantly surprised to find the girls make quicker progress on the trip back. We cross the Sandy River on the bridge, thankful we don't have to wade in those fast, silty waters flowing from Reid Glacier on Mt. Hood. The trail follows an old road for a time then turns back toward the river. The girls navigate this rocky section like little experts. We know we're getting near the car when we start weaving through stubby fir trees stunted by heavy snows. The sun has already set behind Hiyu Mountain and Sentinel Peak to the West of Lolo Pass Road and we're the last car in the parking lot. At 2 and 4 our girls were amazing little troopers. The youngest needed several rides on Daddy's shoulders but our oldest hiked the whole trip herself. We buckle the girls into their car seats and make our way down the narrow paved road back to home. The girls are both asleep before we get off the narrow track onto the slightly wider two lane Lolo Pass Road. We decide we're ready to try a weekend backpack trip to Twin Lakes. The distance is slightly shorter with some steeper elevation and there is a rewarding lake at the end to camp by. All those walks in the park are paying off.

**Introduction**

You have been thinking about taking your kids into the wilds and sharing with them the amazing world of the outdoors. But where do you begin? Maybe you are wondering if your kids are old enough or how you can keep them safe. Maybe you backpacked before kids, you are getting anxious to get back out on the trail, and you really want to take them along. Well, you can!

At first glance, it can seem overwhelming to take kids

backpacking. But the rewards far outweigh the work involved. In this chapter I will answer those questions about how to prepare your kids for the rigors of overnight trips into the wild lands. I will show you how you can get them physically prepared while also readying them for the mental challenges of carrying their gear and sleeping outside in unfamiliar, wild places. In subsequent chapters we'll discover how to get all your gear into camp without breaking anyone's back, how to keep everyone moving up the trail, what to do when you get to camp, and much more.

Kids of all ages are remarkably adaptable to spending long stretches of time in the outdoors. With every little walk in the neighborhood they gain strength. With every exploration of the local park they gain confidence being outside. With every backyard sleepover or car camping trip they get comfortable sleeping in tents and sleeping bags. In an age when children live lives sheltered by modern conveniences we may wonder how they will adjust. However, with a little preparation and planning, kids find the mysteries of the wilds irresistible.

**Physical and Mental Conditioning**
Kids have the same needs for physical conditioning that we do as adults. But workout plans and brisk walks just for the sake of getting in shape are rarely received well. Their short attention spans and lack of long-term thinking get in the way. It is much better to get kids involved with a lifestyle of active living and active play– especially active play outside. You may find yourself enjoying "getting in shape" more than you ever have before!

Our family discovered many a hidden little creek and untraveled gravel road near home when we were learning to carry loads and trying out new gear. Short day hikes and car camping trips count toward the bigger goal of an overnight backpacking trip. You can start your adventures long before you have the gear you need and before you feel "in shape" enough for longer treks.

There are as many different ways to get in shape as there are families. I'll share just a few suggestions to get you started, but let your imagination take flight. Find those activities that your family loves and get out and play.

- Playgrounds are excellent places to get stronger. Swing from monkey bars, climb up slide ladders, and race from one challenge to the next. It all counts in conditioning a child's body (and yours) for the demands of hiking several trail miles.
- If you have it in your budget, try rock climbing as a family. Many community colleges have rock climbing walls where you can climb and take lessons for a reasonable cost.
- If your kids are old enough, go for bike rides around your neighborhood. As they gain skill, go for longer rides with more challenging terrain.
- In the summer, go swimming and challenge each other to see how far or how fast you can swim (safely, of course) to a particular goal.
- Find a place to go sledding in winter. No one will even notice how many miles you have walked up steep hills because you are having so much fun sliding down!

All of these activities can be considered "cross training". Most of us are familiar with the concept of cross training to strengthen our bodies in a variety of ways beyond our target activity. This will help balance your body's strength and endurance. More importantly, it keeps everyone from getting bored.

The very best way to prepare for long walks over uneven ground is to ... take long walks over uneven ground. **Require your body to do the type of work you will do on your hike. The more you do, the more prepared you will be for the actual trail**. There are many ways to make walking and hiking attractive to kids and the discoveries you all make along the way will be invaluable to a smoother hiking experience.

As you take these day hikes, you will answer those big questions about which raincoat keeps you dry and which shoes are most comfortable. You will find out how many layers your toddler needs when walking half the time and being carried the other half. You will know how much food your 12-year-old needs for a day's hiking. The only way to find these answers is through the process of actually getting out and walking in the woods and on the trails.

Even toddlers and very young children can walk surprising distances when given the chance to try over and over again. Kids won't even realize they are "getting in shape" while they make new discoveries on these short hikes. As they grow stronger, make the walks longer until they are able to readily cover the distances you have in mind for your backpacking trip. Give kids their own backpacks that only get used for these special walks and soon they will associate carrying their own snacks, water, and extra layers with independence and family fun.

We live in an area where the winters are cold and rainy. At first I struggled to find ways to get outside in the winter. Then one day I decided to buy umbrellas from our local discount store and had no more excuses not to walk in the rain. Not only did we continue to condition our bodies throughout the year but we all gained confidence walking rain or shine. We learned how wet and cold we could get and still be okay. We learned what clothing and shoes worked best for each of us in the rain and just how many layers we needed to stay warm. Experiment in the less than ideal weather of your area.

We took walks in our neighborhood and took day hikes in all kinds of weather. Don't be afraid to get outside in inclement weather. It prepares both you and your children for the mental aspects of backpacking. You will gain confidence in your ability to keep going even if conditions aren't perfect. You will discover which person in the family needs extra layers, and who gets overheated quickly. You will learn how many snacks are really necessary and which water bottle doesn't leak (even when dropped on the ground or put in a backpack upside down). You will find out just how capable each of you is to adapting to a variety of conditions. You will also set the stage for how you expect your children to respond when they are uncomfortable or tired. All of these experiences and practice will pay off when you are far from the comforts of home. You will feel safer and have confidence if things go wrong.

At the same time their bodies are growing stronger, they are also getting mentally conditioned for the demands of walking several miles. All of these adjustments take time. This is why a lifestyle of active living is the best way to prepare the whole family for backpacking. Find activities your family enjoys for every season and **spend a minimum of three days a week being active for 30 minutes or more**. Everything active counts for conditioning. The sports your kids participate in. Taking bicycle rides around the block. Walks in the neighborhood and day hikes near home. Not only will you be prepared for your backpack trip into the wilds, but family life will take on new dimensions as you play together and absorb the beauty of the outdoors.

**Setting the Stage**
Part of the fun of taking a trip into the wilderness is the anticipation of adventure and challenge. Poring over maps, calculating daily mileage, drying food, and weighing gear are all part of the fun. We thrive on hope for the future. Kids are no different. They just need shorter timeframes and quicker feedback.

Allowing kids to be part of the planning builds anticipation. It gives them a reason to be involved with the process of preparing and builds their confidence as important contributors to the journey.
Involve your kids in the process of pre-trip planning and doing the mundane tasks of getting ready.

Getting kids involved in planning includes them in the bigger picture of what you are trying to accomplish and helps them see the whys while teaching them the how to's. You may be surprised at the value their perspective and input brings to the table.

When kids measure out each day's snacks, they tend not to waste them on the trail. When they help weigh all the gear, they have a bit more understanding of just how much you are carrying for them. They take seriously their contribution of carrying their own gear. They eat their meals with gusto knowing just how much work went into preparing them.

Sure it takes more time and more effort to let them help. It might take you twice as long as it would to do yourself. But the benefits are worth it. You will find them more engaged in the hike and less entitled along the way. The big rewards come when they are teens and can plan a trip of their own and take you along for the ride!

**Conclusion**
With preparation, kids will thrive in wild country and so will you. Our job as adults is to give kids plenty of chances to get physically and mentally prepared so their experiences on the trail are fun and rewarding. Developing a family lifestyle of active living, including active living outdoors, naturally conditions kids and adults alike to the rigors of backpacking and hiking, And it's just plain fun!

Preparing food, weighing gear, reading maps, and practicing carrying their own load connects kids to the deeper lessons backpacking provides. It also insulates them against the temptations of entitlement so prevalent in our culture today. It takes patience and a commitment to the bigger picture to let kids be involved with the planning process but the rewards far outweigh the sacrifice. And isn't that what parenting is all about?

Next we'll discover just what to expect from kids when backpacking. We'll talk about what kind of distances they can cover, how much weight they can carry, and how to get everyone into camp before dark.

## Checklist
- ✓ Are we cross training regularly?
- ✓ Have we built up day hike distances gradually?
- ✓ Are we practicing using clothes and gear we plan to take on the backpack trip?
- ✓ Did we involve the kids in helping plan our trip?
- ✓ Are the kids helping prepare food, weigh gear, and pack it into backpack?
- ✓ Are we having fun?!

# Chapter 3
## Slow and Steady
Realistic expectations for hiking with kids

**Tips**
- start small and keep it low pressure
- keep trips easier than needed
- prepare to move slow
- most kids can hike about 1 mile for each year of age
- kids should carry no more than 10 to 15% of their body weight

The blue sky creates the perfect backdrop for the snowcapped peak of Three Fingered Jack. The jagged peak dominates the horizon before me. Every bend in the trail introduces new breathtaking vistas. I glimpse the deeper, sparkling blue of yet another lake between the fir trees, but I haven't seen my teen daughter's red and grey backpack since she disappeared over a rise in the trail an hour ago. I'm not a slow hiker, but her long 17-year-old legs fly over the trail effortlessly. Sighing, I flash back to her first backpack trip when I carried her in a front pack at 2 weeks old. And a day hike of agonizingly slow progress up the glacial sand trail to Ramona Falls when she was 3... Where did the time go, and when did she become a hiking machine carrying all her own gear plus our shared gear? I smile, reveling in the rewards of years of patience and commitment to the bigger picture.

**What to Expect**
Even as an experienced backpacker I felt a little anxious on our first overnight trips into the wilderness with little ones.

There was a lot we learned by trial and error. Now that you have put in the time day hiking with your kids and getting a bit more fit, it's time to take the plunge and give overnight backpacking a try. You don't have to be perfectly prepared to have success on these short trips. Just take your first steps and enjoy the process.

But where should you go? How long should the hike be? Let's talk about what you can expect from your kids on the trail.

You will have learned a lot about how much distance your kids can cover through your day hikes, but it's still difficult to translate the experiences of day hiking to an overnight trip. There is more weight to carry and usually the trail is more rugged overall than on most day hikes.

For your first overnighter, I recommend you start with a hike you are familiar with. Take a day hike without kids in tow to get a feel for the trail. As you hike, ask yourself how much elevation is gained and lost over the distance you will be traveling? Are there any trail hazards you need to be aware of? Is the trail open and easy to travel or is it overgrown in places and bushwhacking will be required? Is it rocky or sandy or boggy? Is the trail well marked or will you need to use a map and compass to find your way? An alternative is to ask these questions of a trusted friend who is familiar with the trail you plan to hike.

Consider the needs of your youngest child as you plan your hike. **With practice, kids can hike about a mile for each year of age.** This rule of thumb varies considerably from child to child but it's a place to begin when you aren't sure what your kids are capable of.

Kids aren't generally motivated by the same factors as adults, and a little bit of understanding of child development goes a long way in avoiding conflicts and unnecessary trail traumas. As adults, most of us have learned to delay gratification and put up with discomfort for a long-term goal. The younger the child, the less they are able to grasp the concept of long-term goals and delayed gratification. While it is our duty to help them develop this skill, hiking a trail on a rainy day while wet, cold, and hungry, is not the way I would recommend spurring this development on in a child! At least not at first.

Much of what motivates any of us is psychological. Many factors weigh in when considering how long a trip to make with kids. I have found my most reluctant hikers can suddenly hike another 3 miles just because they were spurred on by the competition and companionship of an age mate. A 5-minute pause for a snack may gain another hour of steady walking. Weather, scenery, destination, time of day, how far you traveled to get to the trailhead, how well everyone slept the night before, and what you had for breakfast are just a few of the factors influencing how successful kids can be on an overnight backpack trip.

When planning your trips, consider how much time it will take you to cover the distance to your destination. **A rule of thumb for how fast an adult can travel is about 1 ½ to 2 miles an hour with a loaded pack**. Elevation gains and losses may slow this down or speed it up but it's a general average. Experienced walkers and backpackers can often travel up to 4 miles an hour.

Now that we've got that in mind, throw it all off the side of the mountain. How fast you travel with kids is a somewhat unpredictable factor. Kids tend to be all or nothing when it comes to physical activity. Spend a little time observing kids at play on a playground. Kids are in perpetual motion and then they fall asleep in the car on the way home. Go, go, go, and then stop. It takes practice for kids to learn to hike up the trail steadily and it's a skill that will develop with age and experience.

Always leave yourself much more time than you think it should take. Even if your child is capable of traveling 1 or 2 miles an hour, they most likely will do it in fits and starts. Take the pressure off of having to make it to camp before dark by leaving lots of extra time. Plenty of daylight makes setting up camp a more relaxed experience. We'll talk more about that in Chapter 9.

It is unbelievably miserable to hike at a pace slower than you are comfortable walking while carrying a heavily loaded pack. Especially stopping and starting. Let this motivate you to get your packs as light as possible while still taking what you need. It is much better to hike for a while, then stop, take off your pack, and check out the spider crawling across the trail. Then hike a little further still, stop, take off your pack, and float pine cone boats in the creek rushing down the mountain.

With toddlers and very young children it is sometimes better to send one adult with a loaded pack on ahead to camp, while the other hikes with the kids carrying a lighter pack. This is another reason to keep your distances reasonable, allowing adults to shuttle gear and take turns hiking at a slower pace.

Save new adventures on new trails for when your kids are more experienced and you are confident of their skills and familiar with their limitations and strengths. Then, the sky is the limit and you can take trips you would have taken without kids. Just a little slower!

**What Kids Can Carry**
I took a weekend hike with a friend and my oldest daughter when she was 7 years old. She was a very petite child but she carried her little pack with all her clothes, her water, snacks, and her sleeping pad. I didn't think twice about loading her up and expecting her to travel the 5 or so miles per day we had planned. The elevation gains were considerable and we took our time. I don't remember exactly how much weight she was carrying but I do remember her growing with self-confidence every time we met another group of hikers and they commented on how amazing she was.

Kids are capable of helping carry their own gear. It is important to their self-esteem and character development to know they are valuable contributors on the trail. That being said, it is essential to keep our expectations realistic when loading their packs.

It is important to not overload kids with weight— not only for their comfort, but also for their safety. Too much weight placed on growing bodies can cause serious damage to joints and bones, and increases their risk for falls and injuries. Not to mention ruining the experience for everyone. **Generally kids should carry no more than 10 to 15% of their body weight.** Some sources recommend up to 20% of their body weight, but I would wait until a child is well experienced backpacking and is mentally and emotionally strong in the outdoors before giving them that much weight to carry.

Like all generalities, there is a wide range of what an individual child can safely and comfortably carry. Use your best judgment based on your practice hikes and knowledge of your child. But don't hesitate to expect them to participate in sharing the load. It will pay off for future hikes and it's good for them!

**Choosing a Destination**
What are destinations that appeal to kids? In a word, water. Almost any destination with water is a winner with kids of all ages. Lakes and ponds, in particular, provide a perfect place to spend a weekend and offer a wide variety of activities for kids. It also tends to be easier to keep kids safe at lake destinations than around moving water.

Take some simple, lightweight fishing gear and try your hand at catching dinner. Some kids will spend hours watching a bobber in hopes of catching that elusive fish. Others need more movement to keep them busy. Perfect your rock skipping skills (preferably not where people are fishing!). For older kids, take along a simple sling and learn to sling rocks at targets (just be sure you know what is behind your target). Make leaf boats and have boat races. Take along bug identification booklets and see how many bugs you can find and identify (more about this in Chapter 4).

But don't feel like you have to be limited to the lakes within a few miles of the road. Creeks and rivers also provide hours of entertainment for kids, even if requiring a bit more vigilance on the part of the adults to keep kids safe. Hikes near the ocean open a whole new world of possibilities. Be sure to research your destination carefully for cliffs and drop-offs and take along a tide table so you don't get caught stranded away from shore by a high tide. You can also choose destinations based on activities you are interested in.

High meadows are filled with a variety of plant and insect life. In early summer, wildflowers abound, providing lots of opportunity for sketching and photography practice. In some places it may even be appropriate to take along a backpacking kite to fly in the open meadows.

Trips above the timberline create a different set of challenges but allow children to enter a whole new world full of imaginative possibilities. Did we just walk into Mordor? Does that rock formation look like a castle? Here they find a variety of rocks to explore and identify, and long stretches of views where a string of mountains can be named with map in hand.

Rainforests often offer easy traveling along relatively level trails. Giant moss-covered logs and towering trees offer opportunity for imaginative play and keeping an eye out for woodland fairies or gnomes. Forests provide natural playgrounds with fallen logs to climb on and slide down.

Next we'll discover how to make any trip fun for kids no matter the destination. Even if the weather turns nasty and you are trapped in your tent by two days of rain.

**Checklist**
- ✓ Are the destinations kid friendly?
- ✓ Does the trail difficulty fit my family's level of fitness and experience?
- ✓ Is the trail safe for the ages of my children?
- ✓ Have we conquered backyard sleepovers successfully?
- ✓ Are we ready for new challenges, taking it one little step at a time?
- ✓ Do we have adequate gear for the trip we have in mind?

## Chapter 4
# Distraction and "Just Keep Swimming"
How to keep kids moving up the trail while making it fun for everyone

**Tips**
- find fun distractions to keep everyone moving up the trail
- have a few trail rules that fit your kids' ages and abilities
- be consistent with your expectations
- include other families in your trips
- allow kids to take a friend along on trips

My two daughters are chattering like chipmunks hiking ahead of me. They are 7 and 5. I keep their blue and purple backpacks in view as they bounce up the trail, but I give them their space. We're out of sight ahead of my husband and 3-year-old daughter, but we're getting close to our destination so I let the girls keep going. The girls and I have chosen a camp spot near the lake when my husband and youngest trudge into camp. I'm surprised! I had expected them to be at least an hour behind us. When I ask my husband how they made such a fast trip, he explained, "Oh, we made up a whole monkey guts song!" Later, around a campfire, they shared the song with the rest of us. We don't remember many of those lyrics today, but our daughter still talks about hiking with her daddy, holding his hand and making up that song.

## Distraction Is the Key
Imagine 3-year-old legs chugging up the trail, stopping and starting again, squatting to examine a bug on the trail,

stopping for a drink of water, finally stopping altogether; all this only 1 mile from the trailhead! This is a typical hike with a young child. How can a parent keep the little tyke going?!

Kids have very little sense of time or distance and are ruled by the moment. The older they get, the more we can expect of them. **The best way I have found to keep kids moving up the trail is through distraction.** The younger they are, the more often they need to be distracted. While this can be challenging for us as adults and sometimes exhausting, the reward of getting into camp before dark makes the effort worthwhile. Kids will start leading these distractions themselves if you put a little effort into teaching them how. Soon, a simple suggestion from an adult sets them off on their own imaginative diversion that keeps them moving along in spite of discomfort.

*Word Play*
Try singing silly songs along the trail. Folk songs, Sunday school songs, repeating songs, and made up songs are all excellent choices. Use a familiar tune and make up your own words. Not only will you and your kids be distracted from any trail discomforts but you may also create some fantastic trail memories in the process.

If you are intimidated by singing silly songs with your kids, try your hand at making up silly poems while you hike. How about a story you toss back and forth to each other?

> "And then the frog said…. Your turn!"

If you are talented at memorizing famous poems or passages of the Bible, these times on the trail are perfect opportunities to share your passion with your kids. You can even carry a small copy of something you are attempting to memorize on a 3x5 card in your pocket and use it as a reference as you hike. How about vocabulary words? Or spelling words? The possibilities with word play are varied and endless.

Playing with words is not only entertaining but it makes time fly for kids. You may even find these silly songs or stories or poems become part of lasting memories for you and your child.

*Number Games*
If you and your child are motivated by numbers rather than words there are plenty of distracting activities for you too. For very young children try counting trees along the trail. As they grow, challenge them to add and subtract in their heads or recite multiplication tables. Make up story problems related to your hike.

"If Jennie hikes 250 steps every mile to Blue Lake how many steps will she make on the three mile trip?"

You get the idea! Use your imagination and you will be amazed by the ideas you and your child come up with to pass the time on the trail.

*Imagination Play*
Hiking trips are a perfect opportunity to encourage imaginative play with your child. Are you hiking through a rain forest? Make up a whole tale about the creatures that live hidden in the mossy woods. Let your child take the lead in imagining the grand adventure you are all on and join them in the journey.

*Educational Opportunities*
If a factual approach is more to your liking, then share the history of the area you are hiking through. Challenge each other to see how many animals you can spot along the trail. This is perfect for those times when you need a little quiet! Challenge your kids to sneak as quietly as possible up the trail. Just don't expect to set any speed records when you are sneaking.

You can also begin to identify trees, mosses, and other plant life along the trail. Keep this an overview rather than an in depth study or you will find yourself parked at every patch of moss you come to! Save the in depth study for special theme trips or for when you get to camp (more about that in Chapters 5 and 10).

*Leader for a Day*
Allow your child to be the leader for the day. Kids will rise to the challenge when given the opportunity and will gain a sense of responsibility while learning important trail skills. This works surprisingly well for kids of all ages, even teens. It is especially effective if siblings are along on the trip. A little healthy competition is a great distraction! Just be sure everyone gets a turn, even the youngest. It isn't too difficult to give them the leadership role and still keep them in sight.

*Teen Challenges*
Teens create a different set of challenges. If your teen is just getting started hiking they may take some time adjusting to the physical and mental challenges. Even though teens appear adult-sized and quite capable of everything you are, they are still forming mental discipline and their muscles and joints are still developing. They are also in a general state of emotional turmoil and little discomforts and insecurities are

easily blown out of proportion in their minds. Lots of gentle but firm patience is the order of the day when hiking with teens new to the rigors of the outdoors. Distraction is also a very effective tool for teens, but it requires subtle approaches by wise-minded adults. You may find out intimate details of your teens' life you might never have known without the uninterrupted time a hike provides.

*When Distractions Aren't Enough*
When you have exhausted every avenue of distraction and have seen to their basic needs, sometimes all that is left to do is let a child work through their own feelings of discomfort and discouragement. I suggest playing a quiet, supportive role in this while holding firm to the expectations set before them. If they need to cry let them cry, if they need to be angry let them be angry, as long as they are being respectful and obedient. It is important to note here that the patterns and foundations set at home will come to light on the trail when kids are tired and uncomfortable.

While there is a broad range of developmental tendencies for kids and what we can expect of them at different ages, the important information that applies to kids in the outdoors includes how they express their discomfort. Learn to know your child's signals for being hungry, thirsty, cold, hot, and tired. Always make sure diapers are clean, shoes are fitting properly, and that they are wearing the correct layers for the conditions. Take plenty of water breaks and let each child carry their own trail snack in an accessible pocket.

Discerning between when a child has a physical need and when they are being willful can be challenging at times, especially in an unfamiliar setting. I suggest always erring on the side of a child having a physical need. When they are fed, have had plenty of water, and you are sure they are as comfortable as possible with the conditions of the hike then don't be afraid to challenge them to continue on and "just keep swimming". They will learn quickly that while their needs will be met they are also expected to trudge on with the group.

**Rules for the Trail**
This brings us to the importance of having rules for the trail. Our family has some basic rules that apply to every trip we take and then each trail has rules unique to the needs of that particular trail. Trail leaders are required to always stop and wait for the group at any trail junction or water crossing. As they get older and gain experience we adapt the rules to fit their needs. Running is forbidden, especially when carrying packs, unless our purpose is a trail run. And everyone has to stay on the trail, no cutting switchbacks or making shortcuts. Our approach has always been to explain why we have the rules we do. We find these to be perfect opportunities for educating our kids about causing erosion on the trails, preventing anyone from getting lost, being safe when crossing water, and trusting Mom and Dad to know what is best even when the kids don't understand all the details.

**Peer Motivation**
Time passes more quickly for most of us when we're engaged with people we enjoy. Including other families in your trips can be enjoyable for everyone. School age children may benefit from taking along a friend. Especially teens. Choose your companions wisely! Be sure the other family has like-minded goals and expectations of their children. Each family needs to be properly prepared with

equipment and food so that everyone has fun. It is helpful to share major equipment and lighten each adult's load too.

Children of all ages can cover an amazing amount of ground if adults provide the proper support for them. As in all things related to parenting, a little creativity goes a long way. Have reasonable expectations and be consistent. And don't forget the value of being a good role model and example to your kids of how to persevere in the face of discomfort and challenges. Sometimes helping keep kids moving and in good spirits is more exhausting than the actual physical challenges of hiking. But over time and with consistency and humility on the part of adults, kids will learn to keep moving no matter what the conditions are. You may find them motivating and encouraging you!

**Checklist**
- ✓ Have we prepared some fun trail distractions?
- ✓ Have we established reasonable trail rules?
- ✓ Are we consistently expecting our kids to "just keep swimming"?
- ✓ Have we found another family with like-minded goals to hike with?
- ✓ Are we being good role models when we are uncomfortable and tired ourselves?

## Chapter 5
# Wildflowers and Zoology
Trips with a special focus

**Tips**
- choose a trip focus
- explore different creative focuses such as photography, painting, orienteering, etc.
- develop survival and outdoor skills
- let kids plan trips with a focus they choose

The sun is warm and the early summer wildflowers are brilliant. Our daughters are busy building shelters from windfall wood they find on the ground. Their dad is busy teaching them to avoid rotten wood and how to tie knots that will hold. He teaches them how to identify where the weather will blow in from and how to orient their shelters away from the wind. Our youngest records all the activity with her camera. Later, all three girls sleep in their shelters. This trip is building skills and memories for all of us.

Choosing a special focus for a hiking trip is a fun way of getting kids engaged. Take advantage of a special interest your kids show in things of the outdoors or introduce them to something new.

**Capturing Beauty**
Photography can provide a fun focus for hiking trips. The beauty of digital photography is the freedom to let kids take as many pictures as they want. When choosing a backpacking trip to take, keep in mind the possible sights

you will see and provide some structure for their photography focus. While random photography can be fun and provide a creative outlet, providing structure will keep them engaged over a longer period of time. Give them photo assignments to encourage their creativity. Some ideas are; looking for opposites, shadows, something hidden, something tiny, something huge. Have them make a photo documentary of your adventures. Experiment with different settings on your camera to see what effects are produced. When you get home take the time to pick your favorite photos and put them into special scrapbooks.

If you have a budding cinematographer, let them develop a mini script and then film it on location. Most digital cameras have adequate video abilities to provide hours of fun for kids. Just remember to take along lots of extra batteries and plenty of memory storage! There are also numerous portable charging sources available. Consider a solar charger for longer trips. Use simple video editing software when you get back home and create a movie short of your trip. Then let your kids invite friends and family over for popcorn and a movie night. They will be the star of the show.

Photography and filming may be the encouragement your kids need to develop a love for outdoor adventures. Soon they will be clambering for more trips and find plenty of motivation for hiking long distances carrying their own gear. You may even launch your child on a lifelong love of capturing the world through a camera lens or even a career in photography.

Sketching is another way to provide a focus for your backpacking trips. Trips focused on creating art pieces are a great way to take advantage of a destination with a view. A simple and lightweight setup of a few sketching tools is inexpensive to collect and not too demanding to carry. Watercolors are perfect for sketching in the outdoors. A postcard sized watercolor block of paper is packable and keeps paper stretched and ready for use. A small 3x5 or 8x5 sketchbook and a couple of sketching pencils provides hours of possibilities for young artists.

Sketching trips require more time to sit and take in your surroundings. Keep this in mind when planning your trip and keep your kids involved in the planning so they know the goals. Plan to hike steadily to the location you have in mind with the reward of stopping and taking time to get out your art supplies and create mini masterpieces. You can decide to have long lunch breaks mid-day at a viewpoint, starting your hike earlier in the day and planning to get into camp later in the day. Or hike through to your evening campsite to give yourself plenty of time to capture the stunning vistas found there. Keep camp set up simple if this is the kind of trip you plan (more on setting up camp in Chapter 9). Plan to spend a whole day at your destination with no hurry to move on.

**Nature Study**
Learning orienteering skills as a family is not only a lot of fun but also a very practical and useful skill in the outdoors. Start simple with a map of your trail and a compass. Get familiar with using a compass (see chapter 13), identifying which direction you are traveling, and lining that up with the map of your area. Eventually you can do deeper studies and learn about declination, azimuths, taking a bearing, and more. When your skills increase and your kids are up to the physical challenge, there are endless possibilities with this skill. You can venture off trail and travel cross country to

un-named lakes and ridge tops. You can join a local orienteering club and compete with others in finding your way through a course to specific goals. These usually take place in local parks and are a great way to hone wilderness skills and stay physically fit off the trail.

Nature identification trips are challenging and educational, and teach children a deeper awareness and appreciation of their surroundings. Take along a portable field guide and learn to identify the plants and flowers along the trail and around camp. Many kids are fascinated by bugs. There are many portable field guides available to bring along to build your entomology knowledge. You can identify animal tracks and discover details about their habits and habitat needs. Take the time to stop and study these details about animals as a zoologist would. If you are traveling above timberline or in desert canyons, it can be fun to explore the different types of rocks and soils. In any wilderness, the opportunities for learning about your environment are varied and plentiful. You can combine these explorations with sketching or photography too. You may be inspiring a future botanist, geologist, or wildlife expert.

Backpacking trips are perfect opportunities to learn wild foraging. Start with easy to identify berries in your area. Then learn about the abundant edible plants. Eventually venture into gathering wild mushrooms. Take a class or spend time with someone knowledgeable and be sure you know what you are gathering before you eat anything! The variety and availability of wild foods is surprising and abundant, and kids become experts very quickly. As with most things in the wild, **use common sense and don't take chances when it comes to eating wild plants.** Watch out for plants that cause skin irritation such as nettles, poison oak, or poison ivy. Learn to identify and avoid these. Be sure to establish common sense boundaries with your kids, too, that fit their ages. Our family rule is no one eats anything unless a parent identifies it first. We are able to flex this rule as our kids learn to clearly identify certain plants. For instance, my kids readily know how to identify several wild berries and the tart, clover-leaf shaped wood sorrel (oxalis). These plants are free for their use.

**Outdoor Challenges**
If your family enjoys physical challenges or competition, you can make almost any part of a backpacking trip a challenge. See who can sneak through the woods silently and get closest to a parent stationed in a central place. Go swimming in the crystal waters of mountain lakes or climb high peaks.

As kids get older and gain independence in carrying their own gear, challenge them to be self-sustaining and see how little they actually need to have fun and be comfortable and safe. Try multi-day trips with increasing distances. There are as many options for this as there are families who create them!
When you and your family try new things and add challenges to your adventures, it's wise to have a bail-out plan that allows you to get safely out of the wilderness if the distance or challenge proves too great. Study maps of your trip area and find the closest exit routes. The alternatives may be as simple as staying in one camp area longer than you had planned because it isn't fun to push distances anymore. Communicate these possibilities and alternate plans with your emergency contacts at home so everyone knows what to expect.

The great outdoors provides endless opportunities for many different kinds of exploration and activities. Find those that best fit your family and you will have many years of fun and memories.

**Checklist**
- ✓ Have we talked about activities we would like to try outdoors?
- ✓ Are we listening for and observing our kids' interests?
- ✓ Are we giving them new ideas to explore?
- ✓ Are we making sure we're educated enough to keep everyone safe?
- ✓ Do we have a backup plan to keep things safe and fun?
- ✓ Have we communicated our backup plan with our emergency contacts at home?

# Chapter 6
# Soup, Nuts, and the Kitchen Sink
Well-fed kids are happy hikers

**Tips**
- research different approaches to packing backpacking food
- experiment to find what fits your family's needs and budget
- try drying foods at home to save weight, money, and make what you like best
- avoid foods that melt or spoil in heat
- choose nutrient dense foods to save weight

"Measure ½ cup of almonds into snack bags, one for each day. And don't forget to check the food dryer and see if the pears are dry." The sweet smell of drying pears fills the house, and presoaked almonds are freshly roasted and cooling on the counter. Zip bags of food are stacked neatly in piles for each person, divided into snacks, breakfasts, lunches, and dinners. Everything is weighed on a kitchen scale and each portion is measured carefully. After years of experimenting and practice, we now carry less than 1.5 pounds of food per person per day on the trail. We have lots of variety and are filled with energy each day. The kids help with every step and they know just how much work goes into the preparation and planning.

Carrying and preparing good food in the wilderness can seem daunting, but with a little planning, good nutrition on the trail is not difficult. I have been experimenting with different ideas and methods for years and now I feel we have a good system that works for our family. Every family has to find what works best for them based on the dietary and nutritional needs of each member. There are many ways to approach this but I've found a few that didn't work well and some that do.

The standard for weight to carry is 2 to 2.5 pounds of food per day per person. As I stated above, we have been able to reduce that to 1.5 pounds per day while also increasing nutrient value. If you choose any of the more standard approaches to backpacking food, you will need to plan for the greater weight to get the nutrition needed on the trail.

Commercial freeze dried backpacking foods may seem like a lightweight, convenient idea but the reality is they tend to be heavy when compared to home prepared foods and are nutritionally inferior. They are very expensive, especially when considering feeding a family. And the taste... let's just say, there is no comparison to homemade! They are also bound to cause tummy troubles. Use with caution. You can start here and then replace dinners as you learn to create your own. The longer your trips become, the more important weight and nutrition are.

Another recommendation commonly found in backpacking books, is to buy "quick to prepare" foods from your grocery store. Dried soup mixes, instant rice and oatmeal, soup-in-a-plastic-cup, pasta in a cardboard bowl, anything you can just add boiling water to. Combine with some good old raisins and peanuts in a bag and you are good to go. This can work and I've done it, but the end result was losing energy day by day on the trail and growing weary of food tasting the same day in and day out. You can combine this approach with more nutrient dense meals as you discover how to prepare them and what your family will eat.

I've found the best approach is to make all my backpacking food at home. This is especially important when feeding kids. It is important to provide familiar, nutritious foods when backpacking with kids. Out on the trail is not the time to introduce new foods and tastes. It is already an insecure setting for kids and familiar, nutritious food goes a long way in making the experience wonderful. It is OK to ease into this if you aren't experienced preserving your own food. Start with one good homemade meal on a weekend trip. Then make two and so on until you feel confident preparing all your backpacking food at home.

You will need a food dryer. Borrow from a friend or family member. Or buy one from the small appliance section of your local chain store. You don't need a top-of-the-line dryer or anything fancy. A simple, inexpensive dryer with stacking trays is sufficient for preparing backpacking foods. If you can't get your hands on a food dryer then you can do everything described here in your oven. It just takes longer and requires more vigilance on your part.

The beauty of drying your own food at home is you can transform your kids' favorite meals into easy to carry and easy to fix food for the trail. Soups, stew, stir-fry, omelets, spaghetti are all fair game for whole meals dried and ready to add boiling water and enjoy in the wilds. Our family prefers to sacrifice a bit of variety for simplicity. We can do this because our food is very nutrient dense, delicious, and satisfying.

## Breakfast
For breakfast we enjoy a hot cereal made of masa harina. It cooks quickly in a pot cozy and is delicious. It will sustain us if we add at least one tablespoon of coconut oil per serving, chopped nuts, and dried fruit. A tiny bit of maple syrup is delicious but not necessary. You can do the same with quick cook rolled oats. We eat a primarily grain free diet now so our newest experiment is drying our favorite omelet and frittata combinations in the food dryer. They require simple rehydration in a pot cozy with boiling water. You can make "cereal" bars if firing up your cook stove in the morning is just too much effort.

## Snacks
Snacks are an important part of trail nutrition and should be hearty and nutrient dense. Dried fruits, roasted nuts and seeds, jerky, and fruit leather are usually what are in our packs. There are so many combinations you can come up with to create endless variety! Our favorite way to fix snacks is to measure out nuts, seeds, fruit, and jerky for the day in separate bags and then combine them on the trail. This allows us to have whatever variety we are craving for that day. Then whatever is left over (if there is any!) can be mixed in one of the bags and saved for a day we're particularly hungry.

Candy doesn't have to be forbidden if your family includes some sugar in your diet, but we find we rarely want it on the trail. A little dark chocolate is a nice treat but has to be stored deep in your pack or it melts into a gooey mess in the heat of the day. Homemade cookies and bars make great treats and are nutritious when you make them at home. It's OK to include treats your family finds comforting.

Jerky and pemmican are simple to make at home in your oven or food dryer. It's as easy as soaking thinly sliced meat in a marinade for a few hours then drying it on a cookie sheet in the oven or on the trays of your food dryer. Our favorite marinade is tamari. That's it! Just beef or venison soaked in tamari. You can get very elaborate with jerky recipes, but try to avoid getting it too salty.

**Lunch**
Lunch is a challenging meal on the trail. Usually you don't want to take the time to stop and cook. It is possible to extend your snacks to include lunch. While I have done it this way before, I have found on longer trips it is nice to have something a little different than what I'm eating as I hike up the trail. When the weather is cold, stop and boil water to make some instant soup for lunch. Your kids will be happier trail troopers in the afternoon and camp set up in the evening will go much smoother.

Pita bread, salami, hard cheeses, string cheese, bagels, peanut butter in tubes, foil packaged tuna, salmon, or chicken are all good options for lunch. It is an easy meal to prepare ahead of time, but it also is one of the heaviest. Use your heaviest foods on the first day or two of your trip. Don't be afraid to experiment with new ideas. Scour your grocery store for inspiration. You may discover something new!

**Dinner**
If we could carry only one food on our backpacking trips (or any other kinds of outdoor adventure) it would be pemmican. This traditional Native American food is extremely nutrient dense per pound, easy to carry, and satisfying. You won't find pemmican in most stores. There

are a few places to order it online but it's quite expensive. With a little planning it isn't hard to make at home. The ingredients are simply rendered fat and dried, powdered meat in approximately 50/50 proportions.

I was able to get grass-fed beef fat from my local health food store for cheap. I put the fat in an oven proof pan in the oven on low heat and left it until the fat was thoroughly melted away from any meat. I also do this on the stove top in a heavy pan but I find the oven produces a better result. You don't want to overheat the fat or it will turn dark and have a burnt taste. Pour off the melted fat into a glass jar. The left over "cracklin's" that separate from the rendered fat will leave your pets drooling.

I dry thinly sliced raw meat in the food dryer or oven just like for jerky except without the marinade. When thoroughly dry I pulverize it in a blender or food processor until powdery. Then I mix equal portions of fat and powdered meat until all the meat is covered in the fat. This is not an exact measure and I usually add melted fat slowly to the dried meat until it sticks together.

There are two ways you can go with seasoning pemmican. We make savory pemmican with lots of herbs, spices and salt that we use for our dinners. We also make a sweet pemmican for snacking, with dried berries, chopped nuts, and maple syrup. The sweet pemmican required a lot of experimenting to get something everyone enjoys. Be careful to not overdo the fat in the sweet pemmican to make it more palatable. I try to put just enough to keep it from being crumbly and add lots of dried berries and chopped nuts.

Savory pemmican is the basis of our hearty dinners in camp. With plenty of healthy fat to keep us energized and warm, we find it immensely satisfying. We make our savory pemmican strong flavored. When boiling water is added it will dilute the flavors. We bag a variety of home dried vegetables in small zip bags and then each evening in camp add whatever sounds good to our pot cozy with 2 cups of boiling water. For a starch, we either add dried potatoes, dried squash, or dried yams or sweet potatoes. The family favorite is dried potatoes but the other starches add variety. We use either instant potatoes or our own home dried potatoes. Both work equally well.

This style of dinner is extremely hearty and healthy and we never seem to tire of it. But it is also very simple to cook your favorite dinner at home, dry individual portions (about 2 or 3 cups) in a food dryer and then rehydrate on the trail. The trick to getting this to turn out just like at home is to weigh the food before putting it into the dryer and make a note. After the food is dried, weigh it again and subtract from the original weight. Write the difference on the zip bag. Then in camp add boiling water, in the amount of the difference you wrote on the bag, to the dried food. It will turn out just like you had made it fresh at home. Try spaghetti, stew, and hearty soups.

Quality whole grain pasta with packaged sauces make good dinners. Pasta is quick to cook, but honestly very messy to clean up after in camp. You can buy freeze dried vegetables and meats and add to quick cook rice. Add more water for hearty soup or less water for a casserole style meal. There are many ways to make nutritious and satisfying dinners. Experiment to find what fits your family's needs and tastes.

## Trail Drinks

I've experimented with a variety of trail drinks over the years. There are many sugary powdered drinks that are easy to add to a water bottle. We tend to avoid sugar, so I've eliminated them but they have their place in keeping reluctant drinkers hydrated. Powdered electrolyte mixes can be helpful, also, and there is a wide variety of flavors and quality. Do your research and experiment to find what fits your needs. As we work on nutrition at home, we also try to carry it over to our outdoor adventures. Good, clean water is the best drink while hiking.

Hot drinks are important in the outdoors! In the morning a hot cup of tea or coffee gets you warmed up and moving. At night high fat hot drinks can help you sleep warmer and energize you after a long day of hiking. We make exceptions to sugar to include hot cocoa in our evening meals. Try your hand at making your own and you can choose the ingredients!

Nutrient dense food helps to lighten your load. However, if there is any place I am willing to splurge and carry more weight; it is in the area of food. The experience we are trying to build with our kids needs to be fun! Taking along foods they enjoy can help accomplish the goal of a fun trip. Every part of our trips should be memorable and the food we take is no exception. This can be especially helpful on multi-day trips.

Food is also a consumable, meaning your packs will get lighter with each meal. Generally what I do is plan to take heavier fresh foods for the first couple of days and save the lighter, dried meals for later in the trip. This ensures your fresh food stays fresh and your pack gets lighter faster.

A hearty salad of fresh vegetables for lunch on the first day eases the transition to backpacking food. Sprinkle on a bit of chicken from a foil pack and some sunflower seeds to increase the calories. Now that high ridge view will be forever associated with crunchy lettuce and fresh tomatoes.

Suddenly picky eaters may find vegetables a new adventure! Carefully packed fresh fruit is delightful after a full day of hiking. Fresh eggs and a bit of bacon on a cold mountain morning brighten spirits and create fond memories. For the rest of the trip, use that nutrient dense, lightweight food you have been experimenting with. You will maintain health and energy and still carry less weight than packaged backpacking food.

Start with simple, just-add-boiling-water meals. Practice making them in your kitchen, then the backyard, and then out on the trail during your day hikes. You can make a hot meal for lunch on a day trip. This makes an enjoyable trip and provides good practice. It truly takes experimentation to find what best fits the palate and dietary needs of your family. Don't be afraid to try something new on day trips. No one will starve if your experiment flops. Take a few extra snacks for that trip and everyone will have plenty of calories. Be patient with yourself and get everyone involved with cooking.

When I hike with friends, there are as many different meal plans as there are participants. The common themes are keeping everything as light as you can, finding those things you digest well while hiking, and what is convenient to make and clean up when you are tired at the end of the day. Experiment, read, and come up with your own ideas! And get the kids involved in the process.

**Checklist**
- ✓ Are we experimenting with different kinds of backpacking foods?
- ✓ Have we tried them out in the kitchen and on day trips?
- ✓ Are we paying close attention to how each family member is affected by the meals?
- ✓ Are we modeling positive attitudes about trying new foods?
- ✓ Have we weighed our food and let the kids help plan and prepare meals?
- ✓ Do we let kids help cook and clean up appropriate to their ages and experience?
- ✓ Are we having fun?!

## Chapter 7
## The Monkey on Your Back
5 steps for reducing pack weight when backpacking with kids

**Tips**
- start small and rent or borrow quality gear
- buy the best lightweight gear you can afford
- try making your own gear
- make long term goals to get your base pack weight below 20 pounds
- don't be afraid of a little dirt

My black mountaineering pack towers above my head. I can see it in the bathroom mirror dwarfing me ominously. My 5 month old son rides contentedly in his front pack on my chest and I step onto the bathroom scale.

"Honey! Can you come help me!? I can't read the scale."

My husband helps me get the numbers off the scale and I subtract my weight from the total. 55 pounds of carried weight, 50% of my petite frame! I didn't know any better in those days, and it took a lot of determination, plenty of training hikes, and youth on my side to circumnavigate most of the 40 miles around Mt. Hood carrying all my own gear and everything my infant son needed. That trip with a group of friends is one for the memory books filled with adventures and lessons learned, but today I do it differently.

Today I work hard to have a pack with a base weight of no more than 20 pounds and I insist that everyone I take backpacking carries no more than 30 to 35 pounds total, including food and water. These weights don't put me in the "ultralight" category of backpacking but I am much more comfortable than in those days of 45 and 50 pound packs.

Ultralight backpacking is a worthy quest for those of us who live for outdoor adventures. I'm drawn by the minimalist approach and the challenge to see how little I really need to be comfortable and safe in the outdoors.  Slowly, over the years, I've upgraded to lighter and more effective gear, rid myself of the unnecessary, and gained knowledge and skills that give me confidence to take less "stuff" with me. Working to get your base pack weight down to 15 pounds or less is a goal worth pursuing. But there are some realities I've discovered along the way.

Light gear is often expensive gear. There are ways around it if you are creative and energetic, but generally the lighter and higher quality the gear, the more you are going to pay for it. If you have the means to get the best gear possible then go for it! If you take good care of your gear, it will last a lifetime.

Taking kids along means you need more stuff. Not a lot more, but a bit more and the younger the children, the more extra stuff you will be carrying. This is motivation to be as light and as minimalist as possible. However, as an adult I can choose to bear some discomfort and still enjoy myself. Kids aren't likely to be able to be uncomfortable and still have fun. Sometimes a few conveniences make the difference between, "Let's do this again!" and, "Can we just play video games at home?"

Taking into account all factors, everyone has to find their own place of comfort when it comes to how much you need to carry with you in the outdoors. The more experience you have and the more confident you feel in the outdoors, the less gear you will need. Experience and confidence in your outdoor skills for survival and comfort go a long way in helping eliminate gear you don't really need. I've included some of that knowledge here in this book to start you along that path.

So how DO you carry everything you and your kids need for comfort and safety and still keep from carrying 50% of your body weight?

**5 Steps to Get You Started**
Step 1: Adopt a "less is more" attitude and redefine what "needs" are.
In a culture obsessed with cleanliness and appearance it is easy to think you and your child need a change of clothes for every day you are in the field. After all, you don't want to spend your time doing laundry and you want everyone to be comfortable. But experience has taught me we need far less than we imagine to be comfortable in the outdoors.

Having enough layers to keep warm is important and this varies depending on your natural internal heater. I need more layers to stay warm on cold mountain nights than does my friend with whom I backpack regularly. Two of my daughters are comfortable with a pair of long johns and a vest at night and maybe a windbreaker for sitting around camp. The rest of my family needs a fleece or down jacket plus a stocking cap and a pair of wool socks in the same temperatures. Going on plenty of day hikes and backyard campouts will help you assess your family's needs for clothing.

Cleanliness has its place outdoors. Especially cleaning up after bathroom breaks. Unwashed hands are the most frequent cause of getting sick while backpacking. Many times when hikers think they got "bad" water, they actually picked up bacteria from not washing their hands effectively after using the "toilet." Teach good hand washing to kids, especially after going potty.

That being said, dirty faces and dusty clothes are realities you need to accept when taking kids backpacking. The more relaxed you can be about this, the more fun you AND your kids will have and the less clothing you will find you need. This topic is a whole book in itself! Don't be afraid of a little dirt or mud. Dirt rarely causes sickness and kids usually love the freedom backpacking allows to get dirty and explore their environment. Keep a set of "night clothes"– footie pajamas or long johns– so you have something semi-clean to put on them to sleep in. Wash out truly sticky spots on clothing but make sure they will dry quickly. Wet clothes can be dangerous when temperatures dip even slightly. Babies and toddlers need more extra outfits in case of potty accidents and getting soaked in puddles and stream crossings. Usually one extra set of clothing is sufficient. Make sure NONE of their clothes are made of cotton. Synthetics will dry quickly when hung to dry. This is true for older kids and adults as well. We'll cover proper clothing materials in more detail in Chapter 8.

Step 2:  Borrow, rent, or buy the best lightweight gear you can find.
The truth is, ultralight backpacking equipment is expensive and not always very durable.  Our family has often compromised in carrying a bit more weight, but using

equipment we could find or afford. If we hadn't made those compromises, we would not have enjoyed all the adventures we have experienced.

As you start out, experiment with different gear by renting from an outdoor store or borrowing from experienced backpackers before you make your big purchases. Then, when you have had some time to decide that you will be backpacking for the rest of your life, start doing your research. Even so, your style will morph over time and with experience, and you will end up with gear you don't need anymore. You can sell used gear and upgrade. If you have the storage space, you can upgrade and save your old gear for your kids to use and friends to borrow.

As you collect gear for your hike, start with the big 3: Shelter, Kitchen, and Clothing.
Shelter includes what you sleep in, what you sleep under, and how you carry it. This is your sleeping bag and pad, tent or tarp, and backpack. This is the first place you can save huge amounts of pack weight but also the most expensive.

The lightest and most comfortable shelter to carry is a tarp. It may seem less secure, especially when backpacking with children, and more exposed to the elements, insects, and creatures of the night but the advantages of tarp shelters far outweighs any disadvantages. Tarps weigh literally half as much as a tent and sometimes much less than half. One of the biggest discomforts of tent camping is dealing with the condensation that builds up inside a tent while sleeping at night. All those bodies, big and little, breathing through the night leaves a layer of dripping condensation on the inside of a tent and the ventilation just isn't adequate to get rid of it. Tarps are naturally ventilated and rarely build up condensation that leaves you clammy and your gear damp.

There is one exception I would consider for carrying a tent, and that would be backpacking with more than one toddler. An enclosed tent comes in very handy for containing adventurous little ones, allowing parents to sleep more restfully or sit in camp peacefully while they nap. There are many ways for setting up a quality tarp that can accomplish the same security and it is a skill worth learning. But if you are just getting started, a lightweight tent can make backpacking with toddlers a more restful experience.

Kitchen gear can be kept very simple. If you have prepared ahead of time, most of your meals will require just boiling water. Make sure you have one pot big enough for the meals you will cook for your group. When pots are too small, even boiling water becomes tedious.

There are many options available when it comes to the composition of your cookware. Titanium is expensive but very lightweight and will last forever. However, until you are certain you love backpacking, or if you want to experiment with some different styles of cooking first, don't be afraid to use inexpensive and used aluminum cook pots. I don't cook in aluminum for several reasons. In some research it is found that acid foods cooked in aluminum pots can cause aluminum poisoning over time. I would still use aluminum for a few trips per year as it is unlikely any harm will come to your family from such a short time of use. Stainless steel is heavier, but it is more durable and safer than aluminum and cheaper than titanium. Used kitchen gear is not difficult to find and can save you bundles!

Each person needs a bowl and a spoon if you are using one big pot to cook in. Here again, lightweight aluminum is just fine. I would avoid plastic since it tends to die quickly when exposed to heat and flames, but even plastic bowls and spoons are fine when you are starting out. Each person probably already has a water bottle and that is sufficient for drinking, even hot drinks. You don't need very much for the kitchen. A cut down scrubby or sponge and some biodegradable multi-use soap is sufficient for cleanup. A good dose of boiling water will sterilize utensils, bowls, and pots.

Clothing is an important part of your backpacking gear. You need the right clothing to meet your needs for safety and comfort. I discuss the types of clothing you will need in Chapter 8.

Step 3: Create lightweight nutrient dense food at home.
As discussed in Chapter 6, nutrient dense food helps to lighten your load. Take the time to build this knowledge and find what works best for your family. You will maintain health and energy, and still carry less weight than with packaged backpacking food.

Step 4: Practice and refine your outdoor skills.
Learn to set up camp so you need less "house" to be comfortable. Learn how to identify microclimates when choosing a campsite. These are small changes in climate created around groups of trees or bushes. Changes in land shapes, such as small hills or valleys provide protected spaces that make more comfortable camps. Practice setting up your tarp or tent in all kinds of weather. Know how to build a fire even in the rain. Confidence in your skills frees you up to use what nature provides to be safely and

comfortably sheltered instead of feeling you must pack an entire "house" with you. These skills aren't difficult to develop. It takes a bit of study and practice but it's worth the effort.

Learn what basic first aid gear you need and what you can use in the wilderness to supplement it. Take a course on wilderness first aid to gain confidence and knowledge. A mindset of positive confidence and wise caution helps overcome fear of the unknown.

Step 5: Think outside the box.
Don't get sucked into marketing schemes for backpacking gear. Find out what your true needs are and stay within them. Buy the best gear you can afford but nothing more. Do your research– gear changes rapidly in the world of backpacking equipment. Spend time in your local hardware and dollar stores to find gear. Sometimes it won't last long under the rigors of backpacking but it is a cheap place to begin.

If you are the first of your friends to go backpacking, and you can't buy all the gear you need from retailers, there are many ways to make your own gear or use hardware store supplies. I made a pot cozy from items found in any grocery and hardware store. I bought a cheap plastic container with a screw top lid from the grocery store. Then I bought aluminum covered bubble wrap window insulation from the hardware store. I taped the insulation together into a cover for the plastic container and had a very handy, very lightweight piece of gear for cheap. It is still going strong after 3 seasons of hiking. Try something new!

Worry less about fashion and popular design and consider functionality and versatility first. It's always nice to have gear you enjoy but it's easy to get carried away with the latest gimmicks and color schemes. I like gear that blends into the environment and I consider that when I'm making purchases, but sometimes I compromise that preference for quality gear that fits my budget. For example, I purchased a second-hand down coat from an outdoor bargain basement store in a color I wouldn't have normally chosen. But it was the right design at an incredible price.

Following these five steps will help you minimize the overall weight you are carrying. It will also allow you to spend less and still enjoy your experience. Don't hesitate to try something new. If a cheap experiment doesn't work, nothing is lost and you will have learned something. Don't forget to allow your kids to help with these experiments and also help carry some of the weight.

**What Should Kids Carry?**
Generally, 30% of a hiker's body weight is considered the **maximum** weight that should be carried. Much less than this is safer and makes for more enjoyable hiking. Children are much better off carrying no more than 10 to 15% of their body weight, especially in the early stages of their outdoor adventures. Kids benefit immensely from helping to carry gear. As they grow in stature and experience they can learn to carry more and more of their own gear and become more independent.

Start them out carrying a well-fitted child's pack that can hold a few items like water and snacks. As they become accustomed to this, add other lightweight gear. Eventually, get a "real" backpack designed for children and they can carry all the basic items they need for the trip. All their food, sleeping bag, sleeping pad, extra clothing, small "boo boo" first aid kit, water, and their own cookpot.

This is when backpacking gets easier for parents! Be sure to get a backpack designed to "grow" with your child. These packs have many points of adjustment that allow you to change the fit to match your child's growth.

Kids should definitely carry a small water bottle and a snack. This is the very earliest stages of teaching them to contribute to the group effort. It builds their confidence and makes them feel like valuable members of the group. A small Sierra mug or metal cup weighs very little and adds to their sense of independence. Use your judgement to decide if your child is ready for the responsibility of carrying food and gear that will be needed in camp. It is very disappointing to get into camp and find a young child left their pack sitting by a tree at your last rest spot 2 miles back. It's especially frustrating if their pack contains dinner! Be wise about the responsibility your child is ready for.

Sleeping pads are one of the first pieces of "real" gear a young child can begin to carry. Cut foam sleeping pads to fit the torso length of your child. Children don't seem to need much padding to sleep comfortably and can do just fine sleeping right on the ground. But a small piece of lightweight foam pad is an excellent insulator against loss of heat to convection from the cold ground. They become "sit pad" size for adults and are useful around camp too.

We found sleeping bags to be the most challenging gear to carry for each member of the family when backpacking with multiple young children. They are bulky and heavy. Invest in child-size sleeping bags. They will sleep warmer because of the smaller space to warm up and you'll have less weight to carry. I even made my own baby-size sleeping bag out of an old sleeping bag to reduce the bulk of what we had to carry when our children were very young. To save weight further, babies and toddlers can be tucked into mom or dad's sleeping bag. In warm weather this is often sufficient. There are alternatives to sleeping bags as well. Double quilts designed for backpacking reduce weight and allow a child to sleep between parents. Quilts can be made at home too. Don't be afraid to try something outside the norm. Begin by using such gear in your backyard, and refine it before you get too far from the trailhead and the comfort and safety of home.

An argument for light packs, even if you are as strong as an ox:
So, you are strong and young (or young at heart) and you aren't worried about how much weight you carry. Why not just pack in those extra conveniences or emergency supplies? Isn't it better to be prepared? Not necessarily.

I once took a trip with friends around the Three Sisters in the Cascade Mountains back in the days when I regularly carried packs of 35 pounds or more. On the last day of the trip with 7 miles left to hike, one of our most fit members injured her knee. We dispersed her pack weight among those of us who could handle carrying a bit extra and, thankfully, she was able to hobble out without emergency assistance. But a couple of us ended up carrying over 65 pounds for those 7 miles. We were fit and had no problems other than a few blisters, but it taught me that even if I am able to carry heavy weights successfully, I need to be prepared for situations where I may have to add unexpected weight to my pack. This is never truer than when hiking with kids. More than once a toddler or young child has ended up riding on mom or dad's already full pack just to make it into camp before night sets in completely!

When you start out with pack weights that are not just manageable but actually comfortable, then you leave room for the unexpected. What would be a full blown emergency when everyone is maxed out with what they can carry becomes a minor inconvenience easily overcome. Do your best within your budget and experience to keep your pack weights as low as possible. It is a fun challenge you won't regret taking on.

**Checklist**
- ✓ Did we pay attention to our total pack weight, including kids' gear?
- ✓ Are we letting the kids carry age-appropriate amounts of gear?
- ✓ Have we kept things simple and within our budget?
- ✓ Have we tried making some of our own gear?
- ✓ Are we thinking outside the box?
- ✓ Have we embraced getting dirty?

Chapter 8
# Don't Wear Cotton! And Other Clothing Facts
Clothing and footwear for the trail

**Tips**
- layer clothing for comfort and safety
- consider synthetics, merino wool, etc. for clothing
- less is more!
- check thrift stores, bargain basements, and discount racks for inexpensive outdoor clothing
- pay attention to properly fitted footwear

Sleet is coming down sideways while we set up our tarp. All 4 of us are cold and wet by the time camp is made. Even though we're cold, I insist we take the time to set up a tarp shelter in front of the campfire ring. We knew the weather was going to be challenging and we are prepared with an extra tarp. And it's a good thing too! My friends hunt for firewood. We settle for semi-dry wood in this snowy spring weather. It takes me 30 minutes of concentration to get a fire built that will stay going in the wind and sleet burning wet wood.

We take shelter under the extra tarp near the fire. We all have wet clothes to dry, and spread them out under the tarp as close to the fire as we can get them and still keep them safe from sparks. The sleet is still blowing in sideways, but we're protected under the tarp and warming up near the fire with hot drinks. Every once in a while one of us turns the clothes to dry another side. I especially want to get my socks dry. This is a short weekend planning trip for our hiking group leadership team and I packed light, bringing only one extra pair of socks. We take turns feeding the fire and turning clothes. I decide my socks would dry faster if I put them on the warm rocks nearer to the fire. They are wool socks and if I turn them frequently they should dry nicely. We decide to call it a day and head to our respective tarps. We gather up our semi-dry clothes and I turn my socks one last time. I groan and my friends start laughing. There in the bottom of my wool socks are two ragged holes. In my rush to get my socks dry I had let them get too hot. Even though they are merino wool, they have just enough nylon in them to melt in the heat.

We have a good laugh over my blunder, and they take pictures to memorialize the event and to forever tease me with. I was fine for the remainder of the trip with my one extra pair of socks, and we all stayed comfortable drying our clothes near the fire. Clothing designed for outdoor use withstood (mostly) the challenges of hard use in wet weather and kept us safe.

Most of us have a closet full of clothing for each member of the family. We are accustomed to having an outfit for every occasion and usually multiple choices for those occasions. Choosing what to take for kids to wear on a backpacking trip can be overwhelming. How many changes of clothes? How many of each type? Do they need a winter coat? What about diapers? By the time we make a pile of everything they will need to stay warm, dry, to go swimming, for sleeping...well, half the closet is in the pack and any hope of carrying a lightweight load is lost.

Clothing is a simple problem to solve once you know the principles to follow and you keep one rule of thumb in mind:

**You need less than you think you do.** That's right, even adults and toddlers need less clothing (or other stuff for that matter) than you are used to using and less than you think you will need.

The first principle to follow is the concept of layering. Layering is defined by a base layer, an insulation layer, and an outer wind/rainproof layer. No matter the conditions, all clothing needs to follow the layering concept. What each layer looks like will vary with the needs of your trip and the time of year you are going. Even typical summer backpack trips into the mountains will require the same kinds of layering.

The second principle to understand is choosing the fabrics best suited for the job. Generally, synthetics work best for inner layers; lightweight fleece, wool, or down for insulating layers; and wind/rainproof materials for outer layers. One of the most important clothing rules to follow for backpacking is to avoid cotton. This is especially true in cool, wet conditions.

We are used to the comfort and versatility of cotton in our wardrobes, but in the wilderness, synthetics are safer. Cotton t-shirts, blue jeans, sweatshirts, even flannel pajamas are all examples of cotton clothes we wear daily. The qualities of cotton that make it comfortable are also what make it potentially unsafe in the wilderness. Cotton is absorbent and breathable. It soaks up moisture from the body and the air, keeping you from feeling clammy. But cotton is also very slow to lose the moisture it soaks up. So if you are sweating while hiking then stop for lunch, cotton will be wet against the skin cooling you. At first this may seem desirable on a hot day— until you start to chill. Then that damp cotton zaps the heat from your body, and before you know it you are shivering and your core body temperature is dropping.

Hypothermia is a real danger, even in mild temperatures. The perfect conditions for hypothermia are a mild summer day in the mountains, temperatures in the upper 60's to low 70's. An exerting hike climbing to a ridge soaks your cotton t-shirt with sweat. Then you stop for lunch, enjoying the cooling breeze on your back. Soon you realize you're a little chilly so you put a jacket on over your wet t-shirt which helps, at first. After you rest your body, maybe close your eyes for a few minutes, you are suddenly shivering uncontrollably. You are too tired to drink more than a sip of water or eat more than a handful of trail mix. Now no matter how many layers you put on, you just can't get warm. Before you know it you are clumsy and uncoordinated. You keep dropping things and you don't even realize you are weaving down the trail like you are intoxicated. You decide it would be best just to sit down and rest. You can't keep your eyes open and you can think of nothing other than getting warm and going to sleep.

Unless someone who understands what is happening is observing you, you are in danger of going into shock from your core body temperature dropping too low. And the culprit the whole time was that sweat soaked t-shirt, probably combined with sweat soaked cotton underwear, sucking the heat out of your body.

Imagine this same situation with a child who weighs less than 100 pounds, with no extra body heat to spare. It may seem like kids don't sweat as much, but the cotton is

absorbing moisture even if it isn't soaked. Worse yet is water-soaked cotton. Kids are notorious for getting wet at every puddle they come across and cotton simply will not dry out in most mountain conditions. If you must use cotton clothing when you are starting out, be sure to take off wet clothes when you are ready to stop and rest. The subject of deserts is too broad to cover here, but cotton can have a place in desert hiking situations. Just remember that for most backpacking situations it is best to avoid cotton.
So what can you do to keep you and your kids dry, warm in the cold, and comfortable in the heat? Thankfully today there are many synthetic fabrics available that will solve the problem of damp clothing against the skin. Synthetics don't soak up moisture from the body or the air, and dry very quickly when wet.

Synthetics were once expensive and difficult to find for kids, but today most of us have a closet full of clothing that will work just fine for backpacking. Fleece jackets and pajamas, nylon shorts and pants, nylon swim shirts with sun protection built in are all easy to find, even at box and discount stores. As you put together clothing for your backpack trip, read clothing tags and only consider clothes that are free of cotton.

A problem with synthetics is their tendency to retain odors. This isn't really a problem for kids until they reach adolescence, but teens and adults may find the constant body odor combined with a weird plastic smell unpleasant. The solution is quality merino wool for base layers. Good merino wool clothes are usually quite expensive so I generally reserve them for the adults in the family or teens who buy their own!

**Layering**
The first layer to consider is the base layer. This is the clothing you wear next to the skin. Nylon underwear and t-shirts are easy to find in most stores. Our culture would encourage us to believe we need a change of underwear and t-shirt for every day we are on the trail, but the truth is you only need one. Really! Synthetics are easy to rinse out daily and dry quickly even on the body. For toddlers and very young children, carrying one change of lightweight clothes can be helpful for those tumbles into water. But don't get carried away! Experiment on day trips and find out just how little you can get by with.

The second layer is the insulation layer. This ranges from nylon shorts and long sleeve button up shirt all the way to down pants and jacket depending on your trip conditions. For most summer hikes this will
be nylon shorts and pants, nylon t-shirt or long sleeve nylon shirt, and a fleece, wool or down vest or jacket. A fleece or wool stocking cap and gloves complete this layer.

The third or outer layer is the rain/wind proof layer. An inexpensive rain jacket or poncho is sufficient for most trips. You can even make your own rain gear out of heavy garbage bags. They are usually only good for one trip, but they are inexpensive. Rain pants are helpful for keeping little legs protected from the elements, but truthfully, I rarely carry them on summer trips. My nylon shorts and pants dry quickly enough that I just hike through the rainy conditions and change into warm dry clothes in camp. A nylon ball cap keeps the sun off and dries quickly from being sweat or rain soaked.

What about diapers? This is a broad subject that could use a whole chapter in itself. Briefly, if you are using cloth diapers you can't avoid cotton. I found using thin cotton fabric folded into many layers far superior to thick, fleecy diapers. It wasn't too difficult to clean the diapers (making sure to stay far from any water sources) and dry them on bushes in the sun. Diaper covers were easily destroyed when my kids were babies. Today there are many diaper cover options that are tough, breathable, and easy to maintain. There are also many cloth diaper options available. Find the cloth diapers that you can get dry in the mountains. Anything too thick won't dry quickly enough.

If you are using disposable diapers then you just need to be sure to keep them in a waterproof zip bag - this way they don't get ruined in the rain or from an inadvertent dunking in a creek crossing. And be sure to always carry dirty diapers out with you! They will never degrade in the wilderness, even if they are buried.

**Wilderness Laundry**
There are a couple of approaches to this. On short weekend trips I rarely worry about cleaning clothes. I simply wipe off any food spills and wash the clothes when I get home. Kids will get dirty no matter how many changes of clothes you have with you. I just accept it and enjoy the experience.

On multi-day trips it is important to plan time for doing laundry every third day or so. If it's rainy for days, you may have to forgo clean laundry because it simply won't dry. Even synthetics that dry quickly next to the skin are miserable to wear damp when it's cold and rainy. If regulations allow, you can get a fire going to dry clothes out, but keep in mind that synthetics shrivel into melted balls of uselessness at even the sign of a spark.

**Footwear**
This is another topic that whole books are written about. I am an advocate for being as near barefoot as possible– especially for kids. The smaller the foot the softer the shoe needs to be. Do this experiment the next time you are in a shoe store. Find a pair of hiking boots in a women's size 6 and the same boot in a women's size 8 or larger. Now flex a boot of each size, bending it in the direction the foot bends. Notice how stiff the size 6 is compared to the larger boot. This gets compounded the smaller the foot size and amounts to little children walking around on the equivalent of little boards strapped to their feet. No wonder they stumble and fall so much on the trail!

Children transition to soft shoes very quickly. Adults who have been wearing stiff-soled shoes for years tend to have atrophied foot muscles and shortened Achilles tendons that have to be strengthened and stretched over time. It took me 9 months of walking barefoot to fully condition my feet and Achilles tendons. I will never go back! The reduced foot pain, leg pain, and lower back pain that comes with walking, hiking, and running nearly barefoot is beyond description. Do your children a favor and start them out right with minimalist footwear.

You don't have to spend huge amounts of money on footwear, minimalist or traditional. Kids do just fine with a well-fitted pair of tennis shoes they wear regularly.  A good pair of trail runners or cross trainers are sufficient for adults used to traditional footwear. Heavy leather boots cause far more problems than they solve. If your ankles are weak, heavy boots weaken them further. If you are prone to blisters, boots make the situation worse. I hike with a friend who gets blistered feet very easily. Over the years she has tried many different things with varying degrees of success and failure. The first trip she took blister-free was a 5 day trip hiking in a pair of outdoor sandals with socks. The flexibility and breathability relieved the problem. The side benefit was less knee problems because of the reduced weight of the shoes.

Experiment for yourself on day hikes to find what works for you and your kids. Don't even try to keep your feet dry in summer rain. Wear light shoes and they will dry as you wear them. If you are wearing heavy leather boots, take them off and carry them and keep them dry. Heavy boots that get wet take forever to dry and cause blisters.

The important thing to remember, whatever footwear you choose, is: **Wear on the trail what you wear at home.** I can't emphasize this enough. Don't wait until a hiking trip to try out new boots or even new tennis shoes. Make sure you and your kids have worn them on several day hikes and that they are perfectly comfortable. Bad fitting shoes have ruined more trips than probably any other factor. In extreme situations, poorly fitted shoes can cause serious damage to feet. Especially growing feet with bones still molding.

**Socks**
In the summer I hike in huarache sandals, so I don't wear socks on the trail unless the temperature drops. I only take a pair of wool socks for sleeping and one extra pair. Nylon socks are readily available and inexpensive. Thin merino wool socks are more expensive but comfortable to wear in

all conditions. Thick socks tend to cause blisters from overheating feet and increasing tight spots in boots and shoes. There are exceptions to this of course, so experiment for yourself to find what works best for you. Just avoid cotton!

The rule of thumb for clothing and footwear on the trail is **less is more.** You really do need much less than you think you do. Avoid cotton! The only cotton fabric in my pack is a bandana or two. Every piece of clothing is synthetic, silk, or wool. Don't go to great expense for kids clothes. Check thrift stores, hand-me-downs, and bargain basements to find what you need. Kids grow fast and wear clothes out even faster in the outdoors. Be sure footwear fits and is perfectly comfortable and the smaller the foot, the more flexible the shoe should be.

**Checklist**
- ✓ Are we carrying only what we need?
- ✓ Do we STILL embrace getting dirty?
- ✓ Are we adjusting our expectations to fit budget and trail constraints?
- ✓ Have we limited cotton to bandanas only?

# Chapter 9
# At Home in the Wilderness
#### How to set up camp and get kids involved

**Tips**
- involve kids in all the steps of setting up camp
- explore cooking over a fire to advance your skills
- learn basic survival shelter-making skills
- learn to recognize clean water sources
- use biodegradable soap and a simple washing system for laundry

"Do you want to build a fire or filter water?"
"I'll build a fire."
"OK, which pocket is the filter in?"
"The top one"

I rummage through the top pocket of my daughter's pack and quickly find the water filter. I make my way down to the lake, water containers in hand. As I filter water from the dirty water bag into the clean containers I ponder how far we have come from that trip when she sang the monkey guts song for three miles without stopping.

We had arrived at Santiam Lake right at dark the night before. After choosing a campsite, I left her in camp while I hiked back to meet our friend and let her know where we had gotten off the trail to camp. When we got back to camp my daughter already had the tarp stretched taut, had boiled water for her dinner and was peacefully waiting for it to cook in her pot cozy. At 17, she was independent in her skills around camp.

I pause for a few minutes to take in the early morning calm before gathering up the filled water containers and climb back up to our camp site. Images of camps from years past fly by my mind's eye and I realize today I'm reaping the benefits of years of restless nights in the wilds with wiggly toddlers tucked into my sleeping bag, crooked and saggy tarps set up by adolescents, and late dinners while we waited patiently for our young "cook-of-the-meal" to boil water.

Like many things in life, it's usually easier to set up camp yourself than it is to get kids involved, but the rewards of including them are worth the extra effort. The immediate rewards are kids with plenty to do and who have a growing appreciation of the requirements of keeping themselves warm, dry, and fed in the woods. The long-term rewards are teens and young adults with independent outdoor skills.

Kids as young as two and three years old can hand you stakes out of a bag while you set up a tarp or tent. It will take twice as long as it would if you did the whole thing yourself, but they will know they helped make a cozy shelter that benefits the whole family. Four and five-year-olds are capable of helping carry empty water containers to the lake shore and learning about gathering clean drinking water. Six and seven-year-olds can learn to identify the best firewood and begin to learn fire-making skills. By the time kids reach ages of eight to ten, they can work right alongside you and make camp setup quicker. At eleven and twelve, many kids are ready to learn to light a propane backpacking stove and boil water for their own meal.

Every child has their own developmental time-table and each of my five reached readiness and independence in their camp skills at different ages. As parents, we have the privilege of providing as many opportunities as we can to equip them as self-reliant backpackers.

**The best way to guide your children to independence in their camp skills is to practice at home, then give them many opportunities to put their skills to work in the woods.** All the pressure is relieved when everyone knows you can simply move into the house if the tarp leaks, or cook dinner in the comfort of your kitchen if you can't get a fire going. It's also comforting to parents to know the nearest emergency services are a phone call or short drive away when kids are learning how to use a knife or build a fire. By the time you get to a wilderness camp with no cell service and two hours from your car, you will know what your kids can and can't attempt safely.

**Choosing a Campsite**
When teaching someone a skill, we are forced to stop and consider all we know and take for granted. Don't assume your child knows not to set up a tarp in a depression. Sure, it looks flat and comfortable but the first rainstorm will turn that nice flat area into a dish of water six inches deep. Take the time to ask your child questions and let them discover the answers for themselves. How far away is the nearest water source? Is the residue from our campsite going to wash into the lake when it rains? Is there a mosquito-laden puddle behind that clump of trees? What's above us? Any snags ready to blow down in the first wind storm? Are we exposed to a strong wind or tucked into a sheltered spot?

Usually when I camp with kids I'm limited in campsite selection to designated sites at popular lakes and creeks. We don't get as much choice as I would when setting up a stealth camp on a multi-day adult hike. But the basic principles of considering how the environment will affect you and how you will affect the environment still apply.

You will need to learn these skills yourself, of course. There are many factors to consider when choosing and setting up a safe and comfortable campsite, but most of the choices make sense when you take the time to think about them. A little common sense goes a long way in the backcountry.

**Safety**
Stand in the campsite you are considering. Start a visual sweep of the area beginning at ground level. Are there any obvious hazards? Look for anthills, steep hills with debris that could roll down into your campsite in a rainstorm, dry creek beds that look fine now but will be a raging river when it rains. Is your campsite on a heavily traveled game trail? Look for animal tracks and droppings that move through the area. Next, look up at eye level. Are there loose branches hung up in nearby trees? Highlines, clotheslines, ropes left behind by other campers? These can be removed or reused, but be aware they are there. Finally, look up. Are there any dead trees leaning over your campsite? These are known by many regional names but "snags" and "widowmakers" are two common names used to describe trees and large branches that can fall easily in heavy winds or rain or even snow. Steer clear of these if at all possible.

Consider the ages of your children and the natural hazards near you. Is the fast-moving river too close for comfort to let your young children explore? Are there any drop-offs or cliffs nearby you need to be aware of? Are there any hidden holes or small caves that could become a danger? Take the time to look around before setting up your camp.

**Comfort**
Stand and listen to the breeze. Feel it on your face. Is your campsite sheltered from strong winds? A small breeze is often desirable as it is an effective way to keep mosquitoes at bay, but be sure you aren't exposed to winds that will blow your gear around.

Is the site somewhat raised in relationship to the ground around it? You want to avoid any place that resembles a bathtub or shallow pool. These are often inviting because they are naturally level. But most of the time they become puddles or even small lakes if it rains. Consider this carefully. Setting up your tarp or tent in a place that becomes a pool is one of the most common "bad experience" mistakes people make.

How close is your site to a good bathroom spot? Is there enough natural cover and privacy to walk a short distance to use the outdoor facilities? Even more important, is your chosen campsite the "bathroom" people have already been using?! Where are the other potential campsites around you? Will someone show up at dark and set up camp 10 feet away? You can't always predict this, but you can do a lot to prevent it by making a careful choice.

Are you close enough to a water source to make gathering water fairly easy? Ethically, you need to be at least 200 feet from the nearest water source. This provides enough ground to filter pollutants before they reach the water source. If you are near a lake or stream, choose a campsite that slopes away from the water source. You can also choose a site with plenty of bushes and trees between the site and the water source. This also helps filter out pollutants. This isn't an exact science and takes some experience to understand. Just do your best and don't fret too much about it.

Most people like to have a view from their campsite. This is one of the joys of sleeping outdoors. But I put it low on my priority list when choosing my campsite. Consider it a bonus!

**Camp Cooking**
In Chapter 6, I wrote in depth on nutrition and trail foods and how to prepare them, so we will just cover the basics of setting up an efficient and comfortable camp kitchen for now.

The first task is to know how to operate your camp stove. As always, try this at home first, read the directions, watch a YouTube video, and even ask your salesperson if you don't feel confident playing with compressed fuels and matches. Even better is to find someone you know with experience in the outdoors and ask them to teach you the ins and outs of operating a lightweight backpacking stove. The dangers of using flames around compressed fuel in bottles may seem intimidating at first, but with a few practice sessions you will be cooking confidently. Lightweight camp stoves fueled by propane and propane mixes are designed to be easy to operate in all kinds of conditions. Don't be afraid to give them a try.

Set your stove up on a stable platform free from burnables. A flat rock, flat ground scraped clear of combustibles, a flat piece of wood, a wide log, etc. Try to create comfortable seating for the cook. You will be bent over this tiny little stove for as long as it takes to cook your meal. For example, a foam "sit-pad" set on the ground will provide a place for you to sit while cooking and insulate you from cold and damp ground. Take the time to get comfortable while you cook.

Before you light your stove, have everything you need at hand. Water, food bags, pots, spoons, etc. Remember, you have carried your fuel and you want to conserve all that you can. You don't want your stove burning away while you're running around camp looking for the noodles bag. Think through the steps you'll be taking to cook your meal. Be sure to speak these aloud with your young campers and teach them as well. Try to be efficient with your movements and steps, but relax! This is fun, after all.

If you have planned your meals well, you will probably be boiling water, adding dry ingredients, and then shutting your stove off after a very short cook time. Better yet, you'll be using a pot cozy to cook your food after the water boils. This will conserve fuel and labor. While your food finishes cooking in the pot cozy, gather the kids, do a little handwashing, and get ready to eat. Try to make mealtimes fun and relaxed. This is often where memories are made on backpacking trips.

Cooking with fire is a subject for a whole book in itself, but the rewards are worth the effort to learn. Most often the season that is best for backpacking in the mountains with kids is also fire season and campfires will not be allowed. Check your regulations before you leave the trailhead. You don't want to cause a forest fire tragedy or get a stiff fine by having a fire during a fire ban. But when the season allows, there is nothing quite like a hot meal prepared over a cozy campfire. Take the time to learn this skill and teach your kids. It could someday save their lives, and yours.

**Clean Up**
A simple clean up routine is important in keeping camp comfortable and relaxed for everyone. As tempting as it may be to leave a pot to soak for a while, don't do it! The number one reason to not leave any dirty dishes or pots in camp is to keep from attracting insects. In particular, yellow jackets. Dirty dishes are a neon "open" sign for yellow jackets and wasps and other insects as well. It isn't fun to have a swarm of stinging insects converge on your campsite.

Take the time after each meal to clean up. As much as possible, plan your meal size to keep from having leftovers. I have found this pretty challenging with kids. None of us wants to see our kids hungry so we tend to plan a bit more than we think might be needed. After all, the kids are playing hard, hiking, and burning lots of calories. It makes sense they will need more food than usual. And most often this is true. Sometimes though, all the activity causes a temporary lull in kids' appetites. You may find yourself with more leftovers than you had planned.

There are a couple of options for leftovers. If it is food that is easily reheated and you're certain someone will enjoy eating it, it is possible to save leftovers in plastic zip bags. You will need a place to keep it cold. A leftover snowbank, a cold stream, damp moss in a cool place are all options. Obviously this will only be possible if you are staying at your camp until the next meal is served.

Most often you will need to discard leftovers. There are some heavily used back country locations that will require you to carry all your leftovers back out to your car. These are becoming more and more common as more people venture into the wilderness. Very often, kid-friendly hikes are heavily traveled areas. Consider this carefully. If you aren't sure, pack out your leftovers.

If you are in a less frequented area you can carefully bury your leftovers just as you would bury human waste– at least 200 feet from a water source and far above the spring runoff level of high water. Bury in the top six inches of soil for the best composting. Bury in a place where it won't be walked on or where a campsite may be set up. My favorite bury site for dishwashing water and leftovers is under a rotting log. Microbial activity is very high in a rotting log and it is easy digging under a rotting log. It is unlikely anyone will camp near a rotten log out in the woods and it will be somewhat more difficult for animals to find and dig up.

Include a scrubby of some kind in your kitchen kit. Multipurpose biodegradable soap is sufficient for dishwashing. I often don't use soap at all. Instead I gather some wet sand from a streambed or lake shore, carry it to my dishwashing site, and scrub away. This will destroy nonstick pans, so beware. Rinse very well whether you use soap or not. Soap residue causes more sickness than an unwashed dish does. I often boil a bit of water in my pot and pour over dishes to sterilize. It doesn't take much water to wash dishes, rinse them, and then boil to sterilize. You can skip the sterilizing step without much harm. I find it more necessary the more people I am cooking for because of shared germs. Don't forget to include your kids in the cleanup chores! It is a valuable skill for them to have and it's good for them to help.

**Tents and Tarps**
Many stories of hilarious camp misadventures involve a poorly set up tent or tarp. Again, your backyard is the best place to practice. If you are an apartment dweller, find a park or friends backyard to practice setting up your tent. Every campsite will have unique features to consider when setting up your tarp and only experience will teach you to adapt to each situation. Tarps, in particular, are affected more directly by your environment but, in my opinion, the benefits are worth the steeper learning curve. If you choose to backpack in mild seasons when you start out, your lessons will be less severe. For an even faster path to learning how to set up a comfortable camp, go backpacking with someone experienced who is willing to instruct you.

There are many variables unique to each tent design. Too many to list here. Tarps are more universal but have many ways they can be configured. Know your tent or tarp, and practice setting it up enough that you can do it in the rain and in the dark if you have to. Watch YouTube videos for demonstrations or ask an experienced backpacker for help.

The basics relevant to most common outdoor shelters include knowing where all parts of your shelter are in your pack(s). It is common to divide up the weight of a shelter between backpacking partners– it's a good way to carry less weight overall. Do make sure each person actually has the part they have agreed to carry. It strains relationships to get five miles from the trailhead and discover your partner forgot the tent poles. I'm speaking from experience here!

This is another reason I prefer tarps. It is much easier to adapt tarp setup with natural materials. Tents are very dependent on their manufactured design, which includes needing tent poles and even stakes to provide an adequate shelter.

Learn some basic emergency shelter setup techniques and you will be covered even if your tent or tarp fails. Teach these skills to your kids. These are not difficult skills to learn, but they take some practice and today they are often foreign to the average American. A controversial point to make here is that emergency shelters require using natural materials. The common "Leave No Trace" policy strongly discourages this practice. I'm in favor of leaving no trace. However, many wilderness tragedies can be prevented with some simple knowledge of how to use natural materials to keep yourself warm, dry, and safe. Sadly, these skills are dying out in America because we don't teach or practice them in order to keep from "damaging" the environment. There is a balance to be had between these opposing principles. Common sense and wisdom apply– knowing when to "leave no trace" and when to use the renewable natural materials around you is essential to being a responsible and skilled outdoors person. This is never more true than when you take children into the wilderness. Their lives are in your hands.

**Clean Water**
Water filtration and treatment in the wilderness is the subject of many heated discussions. Conventional wisdom is to fear every source of water you come to, believing it is filled with microscopic bad guys ready to pounce on every gut they encounter. This gets perpetuated by marketing

schemes from water filter manufacturers and those who don't take the time to study this issue for themselves. The facts are more complex.

The most common backcountry water contaminants are giardia and cryptosporidium. Both of these bad guys can make you violently ill if contracted. It is true that most water contains some kind of contaminant. This does not mean you will automatically get sick because you drink water that is unfiltered or untreated. Most healthy people have sufficient immune responses to protect them from contaminants. The truth is, the water you drink at home, whether from a municipality or a well, also contains certain levels of contaminants. Someone in a lab has determined that the amount of contaminant is not enough to harm humans. Usually this is true. It's also true that there is backcountry water that is safe to drink directly from the source without treatment.

That being said, you need to proceed with caution. The considerations you must make as a backcountry traveler and a parent, include knowing the risks and deciding which risks you are willing to take. Children are more at risk if they contract giardia or cryptosporidium. The dehydration from diarrhea can have devastating effects on small children. With babies and young children I don't take the risks, and I always filter the water.

Popular outdoor culture expounds on the dangers of drinking water without filtration because wild animals pollute the streams and lakes. While there is some truth to this, there is usually enough dilution of the contaminants to keep you from getting sick. Think parts per billion (ppb). This is the exact same concept as your tested drinking water at home. If the ppb of a given contaminant is low enough, then the water is deemed safe. Recent evidence suggests that most contamination of surface water is caused by improper disposal of human waste.

Common sense will tell you much about the quality of water you are using and whether it is safe to drink. Until you gain knowledge and confidence, I suggest filtering water.

The dirty secret of the water filtration and treatment world is that even treated water is not 100% clean. Water filters can only eliminate a certain amount of pathogens, so even if you use a filter you must start with good water if you want a clean product. As a filter ages, gets clogged, or is used a few times, it begins to lose its effectiveness. If a filter freezes or gets dropped and develops cracks, it becomes useless. You may never know this has happened to your filter. The bottom line, filtration and chemical treatments are not foolproof and they are not 100% effective.

It is my experience that learning to choose good water from safe sources is far more effective in preventing sickness than filtration or water treatment. You also need to know how to use your water filter properly. You will need to learn the area you plan to backpack in. Where do the streams originate? How many people swim in the lake each week?

Are there hidden springs or small streams that aren't on heavily traveled paths? These are excellent sources for water. It is worth the time to study maps and get to know the area you plan to travel in. It may take a very small effort to hike off trail a short distance to find a pure water source. Clear, moving water is usually safe to filter. Spring water,

water coming directly out of the ground, is filtered by soil and rocks and is prized drinking water. Cold, high mountain lakes fed by glaciers and snow are often safe. As a general rule I avoid standing water, cloudy water, or water that flows through an obviously polluted area such as livestock grazing land. Water that you should definitely avoid is water that smells bad, has dead animals in or around it, and water that is an odd color or has a bad taste.

If you are forced to take water from a heavily used lake, then by all means filter it. But remember the filter only increases the safety of that water by a margin. It doesn't magically become pure just because it went through your fancy, expensive water filter. Sometimes it makes sense to combine filtration processes if you aren't confident you can get your water safely clean. Filter then boil, or filter then purify with iodine. Even with these redundancies you won't be guaranteed safe drinking water if the origin of the water is low quality. Take the extra effort to find clear, moving water or a spring flowing from the ground. Know what is upstream from you. Gathering knowledge for yourself will allow you to make an informed decision for you and your family before you get talked into buying an expensive, heavy water filter from a salesman with a pitch about the dangers of backcountry water. Get to know the area you will hike in and choose your water carefully to optimize your chances of staying healthy. Use your best judgement and don't let fear force you into believing what the evidence tells you isn't true. There **is** safe drinking water in the backcountry. Far more of it than you will find in any town or city in the US.

In all the years I have backpacked, taken children and many, many other people backpacking, I have never had a single person get sick. Yes, often we filtered water – always with babies. Sometimes we didn't. Educate yourself and use good common sense and you will be just fine. As with all things that affect the health of you and your family, do your own research and draw your own conclusions! Pay closer attention to hygiene after using the toilet than to the hype around water filtration and you have a very good chance of never getting sick in the backcountry.

**Laundry**
In Chapter 7 we discussed taking no more clothing than is really needed. On short overnighters and three-day trips, you probably won't need to worry about doing laundry. For trips much longer than three or four days, and you will want to know some basic techniques for cleaning clothes.

The most important thing to know about doing laundry in the wilderness is knowing **NOT** to wash clothes directly in water sources or any area where your wash water will run back into a water source in a heavy rain or rising spring runoff. Putting soap (even biodegradable soap) directly into streams and lakes causes stress on fish and critters and leaves evidence long after you've gone. Not to mention fouling water sources for people downstream or who come later in the day to gather water. Carry water away from water sources at least 200 feet above the high water line and to a place that slopes away from the water source. It isn't always possible to find a place that slopes away, so put trees and bushes between you and the stream or lake and plenty of distance when you do your laundry.

Washing clothes by hand used to be a weekly chore for every household. This is still true in many parts of the world. Now days we are used to tossing clothes into a machine to do the work for us and handwashing laundry is a bit of a lost art. Doing laundry in the wilderness is not difficult but it takes a little planning. Gather everything you need; enough water for washing and rinsing, soap, and something to put dirty laundry and water in. Sometimes the container is the biggest challenge. Hikers don't usually carry any container of sufficient size for washing even a small bit of laundry. There are folding buckets available but consider their weight for how often you will use them. When backpacking with a number of kids, a folding bucket may be worth every ounce for its usefulness! No matter how you carry your water, the process is to wet clothes, put a bit of biodegradable soap on them, scrub away and then pour water through them to rinse right onto the ground. Be sure to rinse the soap out well. The most physically demanding part of washing clothes by hand is wringing the water out. Don't twist your clothes too much or you will twist them out of shape permanently. Then hang to dry on bushes or hang a clothesline between trees (don't forget to remove it when you leave). If you are using synthetics your clothes will dry quickly in the sun and light breeze.

On most trips of 10 days or less you will only be washing your base layers and lightweight synthetic shorts and tops. You will rarely, if ever, wash your wool, down, and insulated layers on the trail. If you have spills or get dirty places on your outerwear or sleeping gear, you can spot wash these heavier items.

What to do if you have several days of rain? The only way to truly dry clothing on rainy days, especially several days of rain, is with a fire. Then you must dry them carefully to prevent melted clothes and socks with holes in them. It happens faster than you might imagine!

With some practice in the backyard, you will quickly gain the skills to set up shelter in just a few minutes. You will know how to cook simple, nourishing meals that you and your kids will love. You will know how to gather safe drinking and cooking water. You will know how to keep your clothes clean in the woods. These are the basics of an enjoyable experience for everyone and the foundation for many memory-making adventures. It is much simpler than it sounds. Relax! Enjoy the journey. Even the mishaps become part of the memory fabric and will be something to laugh about after you get home.

**Checklist**
- ✓ Have we practiced setting up our tent/tarp and know how to do it, even in the dark?
- ✓ Do we know how to use our camp stove and feel confident cooking, even in the dark?
- ✓ Do we know how to find and gather safe drinking water?
- ✓ Are we aware of the ethics and process of doing laundry in the backcountry?

# Chapter 10
## Always Something to Do
What to do in camp if kids get bored

**Tips**
- keep kids involved in the camp chores
- take the time to practice outdoor skills while in camp
- have a few simple games and activities prepared for rainy days and emergencies
- let kids work out their own entertainment as much as possible

The rain pelts the thin walls of our tent. Everyone is fed, dinner cleanup finished, and our damp clothes hung on a line at the top of the tent. It isn't quite dark, but it is clear the rain has settled in for a while. The girls 7, 5, and 2 are not ready to sleep. I can feel the tension and energy in the tiny tent beginning to swell and my mind starts to race to prepare for keeping the girls entertained. I can see my husband is ready to snooze in spite of the wiggly kids, which doesn't help my rising anxiety.

Suddenly my husband whispers, "Girls, shhhh!" They quickly quiet down, but the wiggling is only barely contained. "Come look. Be very still and quiet." He points through the netted door of the tent and the girls crawl over him, noses on the netting. They get very still when they see what he is pointing at.

A three point buck slowly makes his way into the campsite, stiff-legged and wary. He sniffs the air and watches our tent for several minutes. He knows we are there but decides we aren't a threat. He continues toward the lake shore, checking out his surroundings with every step. In just a minute or two, a petite doe follows him carefully through the campsite and to the lake shore.

We watch them drink together, the buck obviously keeping watch for the doe. For at least 20 minutes they drink and nibble on bushes near the lake shore. Finally, they move cautiously through the campsite and into the woods.

As soon as they are out of sight there is a burst of excited whispers as the girls share their experience. For another half hour we discuss deer, their habits, why the buck was watching out for the doe, how many antler points he had, where did they go, would they come back, and on and on. All concerns for keeping the girls entertained in the closed in tent evaporate. Once again being in the backcountry took care of all entertainment needs.

When all camp chores have been accomplished and you have practiced camping and survival skills until you can't stand it, then what do you do? And what about those days that the rain just won't stop and everyone's tired from hiking in the rain and getting wet, and all the adults want to do is get dry and snuggle in their sleeping bags for a nap! It's not uncommon to feel some anxiety about how to keep your kids entertained in a place none of you are familiar with, especially when the weather is less than ideal.

I have to be honest; I'm terrible at entertaining kids. I have a philosophy with my kids that boredom is a choice and I usually hand out extra chores to anyone who whines about being bored. That said, there have been times when the weather is unfriendly or the kids I take hiking need a little nudge to help their imaginations get fired up.

**Let Kids Explore**
The boundaries and your level of vigilance will depend on the ages of your kids, but let them discover their own entertainment as they explore their environment. Mountain meadows are rich playgrounds for discovery of insects and plants to fuel the imagination. Old growth forests, with their giant trees, become Sleeping Beauty's home where dwarves are sure to be found. A giant log becomes a fort to hide behind. When given the opportunity to "unplug" and the freedom to explore, kids are good at coming up with their own play ideas.

For those times when weather forces everyone under tarps, kids' ideas of entertainment might not be fun for adults so I've included some ideas for you. There are also some ideas here to spark kids' imaginations.

*Board Games to Beat Boredom*
You may raise your eyebrows at the thought of board games on a backpack trip. Aren't we working hard to get our pack weight down? Yes! But these board games don't require you to carry anything and can be put together with what you can find in nature. Here are some familiar games you can recreate from natural "found" materials:

Checkers — to play this game, one person can use small stones, the other, pieces of wood. It's OK if everything doesn't match so long as you can tell one player's game pieces from the other.

Backgammon — this seems like an intimidating game at first, even with an official board. Give it a try at home and you'll find it's not difficult to play at all. In camp, use stones and sticks much like you would for checkers. Just be sure you can tell each player's pieces apart. You will need to carry at least 2 dice along with you for backgammon. You can bend the rules and share the two dice instead of using the traditional 2 dice per player.

Bingo — with a little ingenuity you can create bingo "cards" for several kids. Use natural materials around you and match the boards to the skill level of your players. Young children do best with just a 3x4 grid. Increase the grid squares as they grow and gain skill. Make sure there is enough material to go around. For example, if you are using alder cones in your "bag" to draw from, be sure there are enough alder cones to put on each board. A single dead beetle won't work well! You can also duplicate numbers on your bingo boards by using stones or simply drawing the numbers in the dirt or sand. There are endless possibilities with bingo and you can include several kids in this game. Bingo is great for teaching plant identification, animal tracks, numbers, etc.

Mancala — Mancala in an ancient African stone game for two people and is simple to learn. It is easily created from "found" materials in camp and it works great under a tarp or tent vestibule. More than one "board" can be set up for multiple players. Create a tournament where the winner gets to choose their camp chore for the day.

1. The Mancala 'board' is made up of two rows of six holes, or pits, each. Make 12 depressions or pits in the sand or dirt. The "board" should run lengthwise

between players. At the end of the 12 pits, to each player's right, create another larger pit. This is the player's store. (Let older kids carve a simple Mancala board on a piece of tree bark or a flat piece of wood.)

2. Four pieces– stones, pieces of stick, tiny alder cones– are placed in each of the 12 holes. You will need a total of 48 game pieces. Players share all the pieces so you don't have to distinguish one player's pieces from another.
3. Begin the game with one player picking up all of the pieces in any one of the holes on his side.
4. Move counter-clockwise and drop one of the pieces into each hole until the pieces run out.
5. If you run into your own store, drop one piece in it. If you run into your opponent's store, skip it.
6. If the last piece you drop is in your own store, you get a free turn.
7. If the last piece you drop is in an empty hole on your side, you capture that piece and any pieces in the hole directly opposite.
8. All captured pieces get dropped in your store.
9. The game ends when all six spaces on one side of the Mancala board are empty.
10. The player who still has pieces on his side of the board when the game ends captures all of those pieces and places them in his store.
11. The winner is the player with the most pieces in their store.
12. Tip: A simple strategy for a better chance of winning is to plan two or three moves into the future.

*Word Games*

The trail games you played on the way into camp work just as well inside a tarp or around a campfire in the dark. Here are a few more ideas for when everyone is stationary.

Telephone — this is a multiplayer game that can be played easily in the dark. The person to begin the game whispers a word or phrase to the person next to them. That person repeats the phrase in a whisper to the next person and so on. You are guaranteed peals of laughter when you get to the last person, who says the word or phrase out loud, and everyone finds out how far it's deviated from the original.

Mystery Writing — this is similar to "Telephone" but a silent game. The first person in a circle writes a word or simple phrase on the hand of the person next to them. That person guesses what was written (silently) and repeats it on the hand of the next person in the circle. This game gets surprisingly complex quickly, so adapt it to the ages of your kids. For young children, you can use numbers and letters instead of words and phrases. To simplify the game, play as partners and guess what was written on your hand from your partner then share with the group and compare your guess to the original. Another game that gets hilarious, fast.

I Spy — there are endless variations of "I Spy". This can be a tent game or an active game. It's easiest to choose categories such as colors, animals, plants, etc. especially when you are surrounded by the complexities of nature. Older kids and experienced players will need less parameters. Use your imagination and ingenuity to make "I Spy" best fit your kids' ages and interests and the situation you are in.

*Number Games*
Many of the number games you played on the trail can be played in camp too.

Guess the Number — choose a number, but don't tell the other players. Give clues to direct the other players. For example, if your number is 45 you might say, "its less than 100 and more than 10". Players take turns guessing. After each guess you direct them with more clues. For example, the first player guesses "20". Your next clue might be, "It's more than 20". And so on. The person who guesses the number correctly gets to choose the next guessing number and give the clues.

Sequence — this game can be simple or very complex. One person determines a sequence of numbers. A simple version is to count by twos. The player choosing gives the start of the sequence, "2, 4, 6,..." and the other players have to finish the sequence correctly. A more complicated version might include, "23, 45, 89, 177, ..." where the solution equals the number x2 -1. Variations of the "Sequence" game are endless and can be very challenging. Find the best fit for your kids' ages, math skills, and interest.

*Active Games*
There are far too many "playground" games to list here. These are just a small sample. Keep in mind your impact on the environment with these games. Choose sandy shores or areas that can easily recover from shuffling and bouncing feet. An established campsite is usually just fine. All the duff and ground cover has already been worn off by hundreds of previous campers and your kids won't hurt the area by a few games.

Hopscotch — There is more than one way to set up a hopscotch game but the general idea is 8 - 10 numbered squares in a line (see image below). Feel free to make up your own pattern. Each player chooses a rock for their marker.

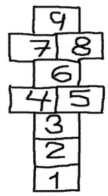

1. The first player begins by placing a rock in the first square.
2. That player must hop down the line of squares with one foot in each square only, skipping the square with the stone.
3. At the end, the player turns around and hops back.
4. The player stops to pick up the stone while balancing on one foot then finishes hopping to the end.
5. At each turn, the player tosses their stone into the next numbered square.
6. Players can't touch any lines with their feet, miss a square, or lose their balance. If they do, they lose their turn.
7. When tossing the rock, players can't touch any lines with their rock or miss the next numbered square.
8. You can assign special actions for a square, such as turn 3 times in a circle, bend down and touch the ground, etc.

Mother May I — one person is "mother" and stands facing away from a line of players. Players in line take turns asking "mother" for permission to move. For example, "Mother, may I hop three hops forward?" "Mother" replies, "Yes you may", or "No you may not." Mother can then choose to add another set of instructions, "No you may not, but you can spin in a circle." This continues until the first player reaches "mother" and touches her. This game can go on and on when players are engaged. Younger siblings take great joy "bossing" older siblings and parents!

Red Light, Green Light — One player is the "stop light". They stand at a distance from the rest of the players who are in a line horizontal to the "stop light's" position. The "stop light" turns their back on the line of players and says "green light". Then they say "red light", suddenly turning back toward the line of players that have been moving forward. The goal is to catch players moving. If someone is caught moving, they go back to the beginning or are out. The "stop light" repeats the "green light", "red light" routine until someone touches them while their back is turned on a "green light". Alternately, if all players are caught moving and are out, the game is over. You can choose the variation of the game you want to play.

Charades — Good ol' charades has endless possibilities in camp. It becomes especially comical in firelight. Just keep safety in mind and make sure no one falls into the fire. You can play in teams or as a whole group guessing one person's "charade". Choose categories that best fit your kids' ages and interests. Charades is a game guaranteed to create laughter and memories.

Hand Clap Games — Most elementary kids learn some variation of a hand clap game on the playground. These seem particularly popular with girls, but boys and grownups can enjoy them too. Everything from "Patty cake" to the complex "Cup" game can be played in camp. Most often your kids will be teaching YOU these sing song rhythms and clapping routines. Some can be quite complex and it's very entertaining to most kids to see adults fumbling to learn.

Ninja — this game has been a favorite of my teens. The object of the game is to make contact with every other player's hands while protecting your own.
Players stand in a circle to begin, with both fists in the center. Someone is designated to give the signal. They say "ninja" and each player takes a step away into a "ninja" pose. There are no rules for the poses except that your feet have to remain stationary until you are "attacking" or "defending" your hands. Going around the circle clockwise from the person who started the game, the next person in the circle makes a "ninja" move towards any player in the circle attempting to slap their hand. Only a single movement is allowed. The attacking player can make a step, a leap, a bound, or any other single movement.

To defend their hand, the player under attack can make a single move to avoid the attack. Once a "ninja" pose is struck you cannot move. Even if you fall down. If a player wants to get up from falling, that counts as their move, either on their turn or if they are attacked.

The game continues around the circle. If a player takes a move out of turn, they have to move back to their previous "ninja" pose and any attacks they made are nulled. Once a player's hand has been "slapped" they put it behind their back in a fist. Once both hands are "slapped", the player steps out of the circle. The last player to have at least one hand untouched is the winner.

Even though this is considered a "silent" game, be warned that it can get very lively with teens and competitive kids. It also seems to be most fun with 3 or more players.

*Games and Activities Requiring Lightweight Items to Carry Along*
If your trip takes you to the beach or wide open spaces, then taking along a lightweight backpacking kite can provide hours of entertainment for energetic kids. Most kites we've tried require a pretty stiff wind to keep them aloft, so you may want to save them for special places where you know the wind will be blowing consistently. But some determined kids will spend hours running back and forth keeping kites aloft under their own power!

A single pack of playing cards provides endless choices of card games. There are many sources of game ideas in books and online. Learn the rules to a couple of card games while you are home to play later on the trail. Or write out the rules on 3x5 cards and store them with the deck. Match your game choices to your kids ages and interests. "Go Fish", "War", "Rummy", and even "Cribbage" can all be played in camp. Playing cards are cheap and readily available.

A simple string can bring hours of entertainment creating string figures. This will take some practice at home to learn the figures, or you can print a simple page or two of figures to learn in camp. There are many, including "Cat's cradle", "Jacob's ladder", "Kitty's Whiskers", etc. String games have been around for centuries and are simple to learn.

*Stories, Jokes, and Songs*
Sitting around a campfire (or even in a tent in the rain) is a great time for storytelling and sharing jokes. You can have a few story ideas prepared ahead of time to share "only" in the tent or around the fire. Memorize a favorite picture book, Bible story, or fairy tale to delight your kids with. Many kids will find it comforting to have a familiar story told before bedtime.

You can create progressive stories, like those you made on the trail. Each person gets to add to the story as it grows. You can even continue your trail stories. You may end up with a family favorite that gets told over and over.

There's the traditional "spooky" stories told around campfires. Think this through a bit, though, if you want to have a restful night's sleep!

On longer trips, you may consider bringing a lightweight paperback read-aloud book. It's a great way to settle kids down at night. Or download a book on your smartphone and recharge it with a solar charger. You may find the extra weight well worth the effort. You will appreciate a good headlamp with extra batteries if you do a lot of after-dark reading.

Tell some of your favorite age appropriate jokes. If you want to carry the weight, you can bring along a small kids' joke or riddle book or print a few sheets of ideas to bring with you. Let kids make up their own riddles and jokes. It's a great exercise in logic and reasoning.

Don't forget songs! Singing together is a great bonding experience for families. It doesn't matter if you can carry a tune. Kids truly don't care. It's fun, and a good way to spend time together. Memorize some silly camp songs, Sunday School or worship songs, favorite pop songs, or make up your own. Don't be afraid to give this a try even if singing isn't a usual part of your habits at home. Just start belting out songs confidently and your kids will love it and remember it for years.

Let kids come up with their own games. You may learn something new! It's likely that your kids know many "playground" games already. If you are feeling short of ideas, send your kids to a week of summer camp. They'll come back with plenty of ideas to share!

These are just a few ideas to spark your creativity. Don't be afraid to try something new. Just being in the wilderness will make even familiar activities seem new and exciting.

As with all things when backpacking, remember your neighbors. Many people come to the backcountry for the quiet. Do your best to be courteous when camping near other people. Especially in the nights and evenings. This consideration often motivates me to find less populated areas to backpack to so I can let my kids be kids.

Another option is to take your trips during low activity times. Take hikes during the week instead of the weekend and during less popular vacation times. It's OK to let your kids enjoy themselves. Just pay attention to your impact on other people and the environment.

**Don't be too quick to entertain kids or be afraid to let them sweat out their boredom.** They learn pretty quickly to entertain themselves and usually do a much better job than we adults can do for them.

**Checklist**
- ✓ Have we included the kids in camp set up and chores?
- ✓ Are we practicing our outdoor skills?
- ✓ Have we allowed the kids to sweat out their boredom and given them time to come up with their own ideas?
- ✓ Are we maintaining a relaxed attitude and keeping things fun?
- ✓ Do we have a few ideas prepared and some simple materials with us for rainy days or when kids need a little help finding things to do?
- ✓ Are we paying attention to our impact on other campers and the environment?

# Chapter 11
## Perfect Potty Solutions
How to take kids potty in the outdoors

**Tips**
- teach kids proper potty procedures in the woods
- decide which products you want to use for carrying it ALL out
- develop your "squatting" muscles
- be matter of fact about pottying in the woods

My back starts to cramp. My three year old daughter is petite but she is getting heavy as I hold her in "potty position."

> "Do you still need to go?"
> "mmm hhhh"
> "OK, well, try to hurry."

Just when I can't hold her there another second, success! I clean her up and show her how to "bury like a kitty." We put the toilet paper in the designated paper bag and then do some careful hand-washing before we head back to camp. Later that evening, we burn the paper bag in the camp fire and start with a fresh bag the next day.

Pottying in the outdoors is one of those things that rarely gets talked about in the detail it should. As parents, we are responsible for the impact our children make on the environment when we head into the backcountry. We are also responsible, and privileged, to teach the next generation of hikers good practices for keeping our wilderness waterways clean and making sure everyone who comes behind us gets to enjoy pristine beauty.

I have to admit, it is one of my major pet peeves to hike along in a pristine wilderness, surrounded by breathtaking beauty, and then turn a corner and walk up to an unburied wad of toilet paper littering the base of a tree. Barely five feet off the trail! When not properly educated, humans seem to have less sense than a common house cat when it comes to taking care of their waste in the woods.

The basics of proper disposal of human waste aren't difficult but it takes a bit of time to learn and to practice. In American culture, we are accustomed to doing our "business" in comfortable, private bathrooms with all we need at hand. Then we flush and walk away. Very little thought or consideration about where it goes or how it gets "recycled" is required. Pooping in the wilderness brings waste management up close and personal and taking children into the wilderness complicates the experience further.

Nature provides ways for human waste to be recycled and broken down into a useful product for plant growth. This is a science too complex to address fully here, however a little basic understanding will help you make better choices about how to dispose of your poop (and your children's poop) when you are backpacking.

The microbes and bacteria needed to breakdown human poop into a non- toxic and useful product reside within the top 6 inches of soil. **This is where poop should be buried**. The good news is, the best soils for composting poop are also the easiest to dig in. Soil that looks like it belongs in a garden, has lots of rotting leaves, bugs, and is relatively dark, is the best composting soil. You can often find soil like this near rotting logs.

Choose a burial site well above the highest water mark and at least 200 feet from water sources. Look for large deposits of rocks and debris along river banks that are much higher than the regular water flow. This marks how high the water gets during flooding and spring runoff. It takes poop several months to fully decompose so you want to make sure your burial site isn't going to wash downstream during the next heavy rain.

Consider how the area you are burying in might get used in the future. Nothing destroys camp ambiance faster than discovering you've set your tent up next to a toilet! Often the most private places, deep into dense bushes or tree cover, lots of fallen logs, etc. are also good places to bury poop.

**The Cat-hole process:**
1. Find a private place that best fits the requirements discussed above. Plan ahead!
2. Remove large obstacles like sticks and rocks.
3. Dig a hole 6 to 8 inches deep. Remember, soil with good bacteria concentrations is usually not too difficult to dig in.
4. The hole should be about 6 inches across.
5. Have your toilet paper and "dirty bag" close at hand.
6. Aim carefully and make your deposit.
7. Place used toilet paper in the "dirty bag".
8. Cover your deposit and the hole with the soil you removed while digging.

9. Place sticks, rocks, and other debris on the spot to help camouflage it and discourage critters from digging it up.
10. Use hand sanitizer and follow with careful handwashing. Just a little water and soap is all that is needed. I prefer to wash after using hand sanitizer because my family is sensitive to the drying effects of hand sanitizer. You can do the process in reverse if you prefer the sanitizer to stay on your skin.

If you are hiking in a group that includes several younger children consider digging a latrine. In most cases a latrine is more work and more invasive than is needed. It concentrates waste instead of spreading it over a large area. But latrines are wise if your kids are new to pooping outside or too young to be reliable in their disposal methods.

**The Latrine method:**
1. Find a private place that best fits the requirements discussed above.
2. Dig a trench 6 to 8 inches deep and as long as you think is needed to last the duration of your stay.
3. Put dirt from the trench in an accessible pile nearby.
4. Explain to each member of your group how to put their poop in the trench, starting at one end. It's usually best to face downhill if you can't find a level spot.
5. You can choose to have a group "dirty bag" or individual bags. Make sure each person knows how to put their toilet paper in the "dirty bag."
6. Show each member of your group how to cover their poop with the dirt from the trench, leaving the rest of the trench uncovered for the next user.
7. Be sure to keep the "dirty bag" in camp, not at the

latrine site where animals can carry it off.
8. Explain proper handwashing. For young children it is best to supervise their handwashing when they get back to camp.
9. If it is raining, it is best to only dig your latrine ditch as long as is needed for a day. Otherwise you may find it full of water. This isn't a disaster and you can still use it, but it can be an intimidating and muddy experience for some.
10. At the end of your stay, cover the entire ditch with soil, scatter sticks and rocks and other debris over the area to camouflage it.

**Packing it ALL out:**
What if you are hiking in an area with no trees? Such as above tree line in the mountains or in arid deserts with dry, sandy soils. What about areas where you can barely find a tree to get behind because there are so many people? These are examples of places where you really must pack it ALL out. I know this sounds daunting and unpleasant. And with all the human waste a family with several small children creates, it certainly can be! Don't despair. There are many devices designed for backpacking to help safely carry human waste out of the woods. It does add weight to your pack. Consider this though, you pack in 2 lbs. of food per person per day and you pack out a bit less weight in "processed" food.

Don't let packing it ALL out discourage you from trying new places or heading into popular areas. It really is a task you can get used to. You have already been changing diapers after all. It's not much of a stretch to learn to properly dispose of poop in the wilderness, including carrying it back out to the trailhead when you need to.

More and more regulations are being placed that require hikers to carry their waste out of the wilderness completely. The more knowledgeable backpackers are about this important subject and the better we get at proper waste management, the less likely we will need regulations and rules. And of course, we are preparing the next generation of backpackers to take good care of our wildlands so their kids can enjoy healthy wilderness areas too.

I've included a list of resources at the end of the chapter to help you discover just a few of the available products for good wilderness waste management. You can create your own poop bags and devices without too much work or try one of the products listed.

What to do with your bag of poop when you get to the car? Depending on the way you are storing it, or what product you are using, there are acceptable ways to dispose of your bag. Some systems are made to dump into a pit toilet found at many popular trailheads. Some are designed to empty into an RV dump. My least favorite, but sometimes necessary method, is to simply throw your bag in the dumpster at the end of the trail. Do your research ahead so you know what you are getting into.

If you are really committed and brave and have the place to do it, you can set up a Humanure composting system at home and bring the bag home, completing the cycle of being fully responsible for what you and your family put into the earth. (See the Humanure Handbook in resources.)

**How to squat in the woods:**
Learning to poop (and pee for girls and women) in the woods without the aid of a toilet seat to sit on takes a bit of

practice. Humans have been squatting for centuries and it's a very natural process. Some argue that squatting is the healthiest way for humans to poop, aligning the colon and bowels for the best elimination. Whatever the health benefits, squatting is unavoidable when you go in the woods.

The modern person has not developed their "squatting" muscles in their everyday lives. You can do squats with or without weights at home to strengthen your "squatting" muscles needed for balance. With a bit of practice you will find squatting isn't as intimidating as it seems at first. Children catch on to squatting very quickly. They require some training in what to do with all their layers of clothing, but squatting is natural for them.

If you are having trouble staying balanced when you squat or having trouble getting back to a standing position without falling, there are a few helpful techniques you can try. When you choose your potty spot, dig your hole next to a log. You can lean your back against the log for support. A better option for getting back to a standing position is to find a small, living tree or sturdy bush or branch to hang onto to keep your balance and use to pull yourself back into a standing position. If squatting is truly impossible because of an injury or physical problem you will need to set up a "seat" from sturdy sticks. Use wood that is not rotten for this project. Find two logs, rocks, or stumps and place two sticks across them for sitting. This will be an uncomfortable contraption but it will keep you from falling into your own poop!

**What about pee?**
I have good news! Peeing in the woods is quite simple and

requires nothing more than a bit of privacy and some awareness of what is around you. Believe it or not, peeing into rivers and large lakes is even encouraged in some areas that are heavily used by boaters. The dispersal of urine in large bodies of water keeps odors from accumulating, and keeps residue from dried urine salts leaving unsightly white spots all over the river banks. These are places you definitely want to double filter your drinking water though!

There is no need to bury pee. To keep wilderness water sources pristine and usable for everyone, it makes common sense to pee far from lakes and streams and springs. Be considerate and do what you would want other hikers to do for you.

**FUD's and STP devices:**
Men and boys have a distinct advantage for peeing outside. Most women and girls pick up squatting to pee without too much trouble. However, if squatting several times a day is too difficult or just seems inconvenient, there are several manufacturers who have created devices that allow women to stand to pee. These Female Urinary Devices (FUD's) and Stand To Pee (STP) devices are handy tools. Be sure to try these out at home first! See the listings at the end of the chapter if you want to give this a try.

It takes some experimenting for modern women to discover the easiest and "cleanest" positions for pottying outdoors. Start your girls young! It comes naturally to them and there won't be an adjustment as they get older.

The same rules for used toilet paper remain in effect for peeing. Carry out ALL toilet paper in a "dirty bag". The same is true for baby wipes and disposable diapers. None of these items will degrade in the wilderness and must be packed out.

**For Women and Girls**
What no one ever told you about menstruation and hygiene while back packing.

Women and developing girls face unique challenges while backpacking. Not only do we have anatomies that require creative adjustments when we have to pee, we also have menstruation to deal with. It is not difficult to adjust to the requirements of managing having your period while hiking but it does take a bit of planning.

Most modern menstruation products such as sanitary napkins and tampons work just fine while backpacking. You may find your body responds to a period differently while backpacking. Higher elevations and increased activity can increase or decrease flow. Make sure you have enough products with you to cover your needs.

All used products must be packed out. They will take a very long time to break down if left in the wilderness and some products will never fully deteriorate. Used products are also an attractant to animals who are drawn by the scent of blood. Store used pads and tampons in zip bags and discard them when you get off the trail.

When using sanitary napkins it is helpful to change them often to avoid chaffing. You are usually walking long distances while backpacking and chaffing is a real possibility. Tampons should be changed frequently as well when you are very active. Find a place as private and as comfortable as possible when changing pads and tampons. Dry out baby wipes before you leave home to make them lighter to carry, then re-wet them when you need to use them. This will help you stay as dry and clean as possible. Be sure to pack baby wipes out! Bury any blood with a small amount of dirt to avoid attracting animals.

There are reusable products that will lighten your load when hiking multi day trips (see resources below). Be sure to experiment at home to know how your body responds to these. Use caution when cleaning them. I recommend using filtered/boiled water to clean these products to reduce any risk of infection from waterborne contaminants.

Take the time to help girls and teens adjust to the changes of managing periods while hiking. With some education they can learn to enjoy the outdoors even when having their periods. Much of this information is not automatically known or heard about so make sure you don't leave them wondering what to do. Pay attention to the needs of the girls in your hiking group and make sure they are prepared with knowledge and products.
If you need to take it easy on one or two days of your period, don't be afraid to adjust your expectations. Exercise is very healthy while menstruating but many women and girls are highly affected by the side affects that come with a period. Stay well hydrated and eat as healthy as possible. Get rest and don't put undue pressure on yourself or the girls in your group.

Be aware that high elevations and intense levels of exercise you aren't accustomed to can cause your period to start unexpectedly. With this in mind, be sure you always carry feminine hygiene products with you even if you aren't expecting your period during your trip. It is highly inconvenient to be several miles from the car and not have what you need if you start your period! Be prepared!

**Washing Cloth Diapers:**
When backpacking with babies and toddlers still in diapers consider using cloth diapers. I tried many different solutions for this stage of life and found large, thin, foldable cloth diapers the easiest solution. For very short trips just overnight or a couple of days, disposable diapers are easy enough to manage. Beyond that and dirty diapers soon fill your pack to overflowing.

Take enough cloth diapers to cover your child's needs for about three days. One day for using, one day dirty, and one day drying. Dispose of poop in the same way as for every other member of the family, in a cat-hole or latrine, or in a zip bag if you are carrying it ALL out. Store dirty diapers in a plastic zip bag until you are ready to launder them. Resist the urge to rinse them out unless absolutely necessary because you will add lots of water weight to your pack as well as the risk of gross diaper water spilling into your pack. When you are ready to wash the diapers, follow the same procedure discussed in chapter eight for doing laundry in camp. The important points being, to be 200 or more feet from water sources and high water lines, washing and rinsing diapers where the waste water won't run back into water sources, and washing and rinsing on soil that can absorb and filter the dirty water.

The diaper stage is a short window of a child's life and it isn't as difficult to manage in the woods as it seems. Don't avoid getting out and backpacking just because you have a child in diapers. Just adjust your expectations to match the demands of changing them and taking care of diapers. You won't regret these trips even though they require a little more work and planning. And you will appreciate your washing machine very much when you return home! In many ways, a nursing infant carried in a front pack is one of the easiest stages to take your child backpacking. Take the challenge and give it a try!

At first glance there seems to be a lot to manage when it comes to pottying outdoors. It may be unfamiliar but it is worth the effort to learn. After some practice the process will seem a natural part of being in the woods. The younger kids are when they learn these steps the less foreign it will seem to them.

As parents we have already had to let go of a lot of squeamishness around the realities of the human body. We take care of little humans and their potty needs every day. Taking care of your family's potty needs and poop disposal in the wilderness is not any different.

**Checklist of realistic expectations –**
- ✓ We have a plan to properly manage our poop on our trip,
- ✓ We are maintaining a sense of humor about the whole process,
- ✓ We are teaching our kids how and why to bury our poop or carry it out,
- ✓ We're practicing good hand washing.

List of Resources:

The Humanure Handbook
(https://humanurehandbook.com/downloads/H2.pdf)

FUD's and STP devices for women:

- GoGirl (www.go-girl.com)
- SheWee (www.shewee.com)
- Magic Cone (www.magic-cone.co/)
- Urinelle (https://www.amazon.com/Urinelle-7-Pack/dp/B000ZZ790Y)
- WhizFreedom (www.whizfreedomusa.com)

Tools for carrying poop out of the wilderness:

- **Wag Bags** (http://www.cleanwaste.com/products)
- **Biffy Bags** (http://www.biffybag.com/)
- **Restop Wilderness Waste bags** (http://restop.com/products/?v=7516fd43adaa)

## Chapter 12
## Choose Your View
### How to determine a kid-friendly hike

**Tips**
- research trails and destinations thoroughly
- DO hike familiar trails often
- be flexible and willing to adjust your plans
- try new challenges as you gain confidence

We started later in the evening than we had hoped. We left home after my husband got off work on a Friday and headed into the mountains. The traffic was heavier than normal, with many people taking advantage of the unusually mild and dry weather of early June in the Oregon Cascades. We had planned a weekend backpack trip with our two little girls to Hidden Lake. I was very pregnant with our third daughter and unable to carry more than a small load. We decided to go ahead with the trip in spite of the late start. Each of the girls had their little day packs and my husband carried all the rest of our gear. Since he was heavily loaded, he hiked ahead the 3 ½ miles to the lake while I hiked at kid pace with the girls.

The first part of the trip was a mile of steep uphill grade in earshot of the freeway. The girls were troopers and hiked the distance cheerfully. Then the trail leveled out and headed deeper into the silence of a huge cedar and fir forest. Evening comes quickly in the deep forests of the mountains and it started getting dark on us. We sang happy songs and listened to owls hooting in the dusk. I knew my husband was setting up camp and would come back to walk with us as soon as he could. With a girl holding each hand, we made our way up the trail in the deepening dusk.

We heard my husband coming down the trail and soon saw him through the trees. When he reached us, he put the youngest on his shoulders and we hiked quickly into a cozy camp set up near the secluded little lake. In spite of the late start and hiking in the dusk, our planning worked out and it was a grand adventure we talk about still today.

## What to Look for in a Kid-Friendly Hike

How do you judge the best hike for your family? There are many sources for hike descriptions on the internet today. There are websites dedicated to exploring certain regions and reporting on the trails and conditions. Printed trail guides are another helpful tool for finding out details about trails and destinations. Many backpacking and outdoor magazines feature family-friendly destinations and include important information. With readily available resources, you can read several descriptions of the hike you are considering and get a pretty good idea what to expect. Talk to other hikers to find out ahead of time what the trail conditions are for the current season. Online websites for national forests, BLM, and national parks have descriptions of trail conditions and hazards to watch out for. Combining these resources will help you decide if a trail and destination are a good fit for your family.

*Distances*

**Consider the needs of your youngest walking family member when planning your hikes.** Babes in backpacks move along at the pace of their carrier and don't require as much planning! Remember, kids can usually hike about a mile for each year of their age so plan your distance according to the age of your youngest hiker and their level of experience and drive.

Then consider how long it takes to hike that distance. This factor is variable with small children and sometimes difficult to determine. Do your research, then make your best guess and leave plenty of time to get to your campsite so you aren't feeling pressured by approaching darkness. If the day is waning, it is sometimes wise to send faster hikers ahead to set up camp before daylight is completely gone. Only consider this option if both groups have a confident hiker in the mix, know which direction to go at all trail junctions, and where the campsite is located. Clear communication will avoid a lot of mishaps and inadvertent adventures.

*Trail Conditions*
When doing your research, look for references to stream crossings and steep drop-offs on the trail (sometimes referred to as viewpoints!). Pay attention to descriptions of the trail going through sections of thick brush or boulder fields. Long stretches of trail along a rushing river will require handholding for little ones. Snowfield crossings on steep side hills may need to be avoided completely if you don't feel confident crossing them yourself. These "hazards" don't mean you can't use the trail. They are just conditions you need to factor in when you are deciding how much time it will take to travel the distance to your destination. Remember, obstacles like thick brush will be over young children's head height and boulder fields and talus slope crossings will take more time with little feet and short legs than for adults.

*Attractions*
Destinations that appeal to kids are an important part of your planning. Will the destination be safe for all members of the family? Will there be opportunities for exploration and play that fit the needs of everyone? The truth is, the littlest members of the family usually dictate the kind of trip you will take. The good news is all those little sacrifices will pay off when they are hauling all their own gear and know how to set up camp independently. Someday they may carry all the extra gear so you can carry a light pack in your old age and you can keep hiking.

We've mentioned already that destinations with water are kid favorites. Places to swim, look for crawdads and tadpoles, and to fish are excellent locations. Other kid-friendly destinations can have interesting rock formations to play in, sand, meadows full of flowers and bugs to explore, safe snowfields for warm weather sliding, and forests of large trees and logs for climbing and fort building.

To keep hiking interesting, it's fun to hike with other families. Kids can hike amazing distances without complaint when they have friends to distract them. Often, camp is more relaxing too, because kids entertain each other. Find families with similar goals and compatible parenting styles for the best experiences.

*Close to Home*
Something often overlooked when planning kid-friendly hikes is considering the travel distance from home. It is entirely possible to take your family a long distance from home to backpack in a new area.

But extra planning and time needs to be built into the trip. Riding all day in the car then slipping on a backpack and hiking for 3 or 4 miles will most likely result in grumpy little hikers, and maybe even a colossal trail tantrum sure to scare the bears away for miles around. The goal is to make backpacking a fun family activity everyone will enjoy for years to come. Err on the side of keeping things simple and easy.

You can set up a car camp at the trailhead and ease your way into the trip. This means planning for extra meals and sometimes taking larger tents for the trailhead camp and more changes of clothing. Trailheads are notorious for car vandalism and break ins. Beware storing extra gear in your car while you are on a backpack trip. Ideally you should not leave extra gear of any value in your car and never leave it in sight. Secure it in a closed trunk or under seats. It is often best to park older model vehicles at trailheads with no tempting items in them to steal.

That said, it is really handy to have a clean change of clothes, bottled water, and fresh snacks you didn't have on the trail ready and waiting in the car. I usually take things that won't be a significant loss if stolen and hide them carefully.

Even better, is to have someone drop your family at the trailhead and meet you at the end of your trip. Then your vehicle isn't parked at the vulnerable trailhead. I realize this option isn't realistic most of the time, but it's worth considering. We've hiked with others who were only interested in a day hike who have traveled with us then took our vehicle home and dropped it back at the trailhead on the day we planned to return. With this option, and an extra set of keys, you can get in your car and leave as soon as you're off the trail. Usually kid-friendly hikes are just about the right distance for an adult day hike so this works out nicely. Be sure to clearly communicate which trailhead you will end your trip at!

Find as many kid-friendly hikes within an hour's drive of home as you can, and hike them frequently. Kids don't mind familiar hikes and will grow in their confidence when they know they can make the distance. With these successful experiences, you can soon begin venturing out to longer distances and more challenging destinations.

You are the best judge of what level of challenges your kids can tackle. Don't be afraid to try something new as you gain confidence. Always have an exit plan for any trip you take. This takes pressure off those times when conditions get difficult. You know you can end the trip early and hike out to the car if the weather becomes severe or the bugs are just too uncomfortable. It is never failure to change your plans or end your trip differently than you originally planned. It's often part of the adventure! Having these plans in advance makes decision making in the wilderness less stressful.

Your attitude as a parent will influence your kids greatly. If you have a "can do" attitude, they will too. Be confident, even if you face things you aren't sure about. Take your time deciding what to do next and **don't panic**. Sometimes the very best decision is to stop, take off your packs and rest for a while. Find a bit of shelter, have a snack and a drink of water, and soon you will see what you should do.

**Checklist**
- ✓ Have we studied trail guides and maps carefully and determined our trip is kid friendly?
- ✓ Are we practicing a "can do" attitude?
- ✓ Do we have an exit plan for our trip?
- ✓ Have we considered the risks for parking our car at the trailhead?
- ✓ Have we clearly communicated our plans to someone back at home?

# Chapter 13
## There and Back Again
### how not to get lost in the woods

**Tips**
- Learn basic map and compass skills
- Develop your natural direction finding skills
- Start with well-marked trails
- Learn to use a GPS app on your smartphone
- Always take a map and compass as a backup

"Line your compass up with the edge of the map. Did you locate north?"

My son turns the map half a turn.

"Good. Now orient yourself to face north."

He turns his body until the red arrow on the compass points to N on the compass dial.

"Now, tell us which way we need to go."

After a few seconds of study he points to the direction we need to travel across the open field. This is a practice run in a familiar park near home. He has a scout backpack trip coming up and is planning to complete his map and compass badge. I follow him across the field and we find the trailhead we've been looking for. He is on his way to becoming independent using a map and compass to find his way in unfamiliar and unmarked wilderness.

**Getting Started**

There are a few tools that you need to be familiar with to find your way around in the backcountry. With a bit of practice you can become skilled enough to be confident of finding your way. It is not too difficult to learn the basics of each of these tools and the special vocabulary you need to become familiar with. It can be confusing at first but it doesn't take long to learn the vocabulary. You can spend lots of time and money and become an expert with these tools as well if you find it interesting. There are many books explaining the use of maps and compasses and GPS. You can take courses at your local community college. YouTube has many free courses as well. Take the time to develop at least a basic knowledge of these tools and you can be confident of keeping yourself and your family on the right path in the backcountry.

Finding your way in the backcountry is not difficult but there are a few things you need to know. I honestly don't use my map and compass very much once I'm out in the field. Unless I'm traveling off trail and looking for a specific landmark, such as a nice fishing hole with no trails into it. How can I get by with this and never get lost? I am being honest when I say I don't get lost. There are several reasons for this that I will share with you.

First, I diligently study topographic maps of the area I plan to hike in. These days, I use Google maps to get a satellite view of the area. My goal is to get the "lay of the land." I want to know what the major river drainages are and the directions they run. I find all major highways and roads and memorize the direction they travel. I locate major mountain peaks, large lakes, towns, even places like mining companies, or remote gas stations. My goal is to fix a picture in my mind of how all these details relate to each other. The questions I ask myself are; if I reach this river should I travel downstream or upstream to the closest civilization? What is between the trail I'm going to be on and that major mountain peak? As I am studying these details I am getting my brain oriented to north and south and where my hiking area is in relationship to all the major landmarks.

With this information safely stored in my head, I can hike confidently knowing I can always find my way even if I get turned around or end up in a place I didn't expect to be. When I first arrive at the trailhead I get out my map and compass and orient myself, finding north and south and which direction the trail travels to my first campsite and any trail junctions I will come to. Then I can tuck my map and compass in a handy pocket and hike on, confident I'm going where I want to go.

Second, I continually check myself if I'm unsure. Sometimes, when I'm hiking in an unfamiliar place, I check myself even if I am sure — just to train my brain. With practice this becomes second nature and you begin to develop that part of your brain that is sensitive to directions and the compass points. I know this sounds odd, but it really is true that there is a place in your brain you can develop to become better at direction finding. I can't point to any specific scientific study to prove this, but my own experience and that of many other outdoors people verify it is a natural human ability that can be developed. I am fortunate to have grown up in rural settings, exploring big areas of wild country without the help of trails, maps, or compasses. I just learned to find my way around. Don't despair if you didn't have this advantage. It is still a skill you can develop. It just takes some time and focused practice. And you can provide your kids with the opportunity to easily develop their natural direction-finding abilities!

Third, I always keep the mindset that I am not going to get lost. I think this is a very large part of why I don't ever get lost. I might not be exactly where I expected to be, but I am confident I will find my way to where I want to go. The key becomes finding my way without walking an extra 20 miles! This is especially important when hiking with little ones. There have been times when I was challenging myself and hiking off trail that I've hiked further than I planned to get back to my camp. This happens often when I'm hunting. I'm going off trail on purpose and looking for wildlife, not mapping a route of least resistance. But I know my limitations and am careful to stay within them. At times when I'm fit and healthy, I'm not afraid to hike those 20+ miles. Other times, when I'm not as fit, I choose to go no more than a mile or two and don't push out into areas that will take me more than that to get back to camp. When hiking with children or inexperienced hikers I'm always diligent to know exactly where I need to go so we don't have to hike any extra miles.

To summarize this, study your topo maps, study Google maps for a satellite view, check yourself often once you are on the trail. Get a good feel for how the land looks from an aerial view. Develop that part of your brain that senses directions. It really is something you can do and something you can teach your kids. Keep the mindset that you aren't ever going to get lost. Pay attention to where you are always, note landmarks, and turn yourself into a constantly updating compass with practice. Stay within your limits and the limits of the weakest hiker in your group. Don't set yourself up to be in danger by going further into unknown areas than you can safely get out of. And **never** panic. Take your time and figure out where you need to go next. Don't blindly push on hoping you'll come across a trail or road. You probably won't. Don't freeze up and sit in one place when there is a perfectly good direction you can take. Think and solve the problems.

Start small when you are learning to navigate in the backcountry. Often hikes that are just right for kids are also well marked and simple to navigate. You still need to study your maps ahead of time and take a map and compass with you. Identify the trail numbers you plan to travel. Take note of all trail junctions and which trail you need to take. It is best to know the compass direction your trail travels from the junction in case the trail sign is knocked down or missing. Mark your trail on the map with a highlighter. This makes it easy to read even in low light. I write all my trail numbers, junctions, and distances of travel on a 3x5 card when I have several trail changes on a backpacking trip. This gives me a handy reference to check when I come to a trail junction. When I'm hiking with a group, I make one for each person. You can do this for your kids as they get old enough and more experienced in the backcountry. I always recommend kids (or adults who are new to backpacking) wait for the rest of the group at all trail junctions just to be safe. I know of situations where families ended up separated for the night because they took different directions at a trail junction.

**Navigation Tools**

Most modern smartphones have user friendly GPS apps that make finding your way in the woods a cinch. Remember that phone batteries die, phones can get broken, and cell service be unreliable. It is wise to have a map and compass as a backup. Practice using the GPS app in your neighborhood so you become familiar with it. You will need a reliable way to charge your phone if you are using it to navigate. There are many charging devices on the market that can be recharged at home or even by a small solar panel while backpacking. You can also purchase a dedicated GPS unit. Some of these have a learning curve so be sure you know how to operate your specific device. The advantage of a dedicated GPS unit is that you can usually carry spare batteries for them instead of needing to charge them as you would a phone. The disadvantages are the added weight and bulk of another item in your pack. You will still need to be familiar with map and compass basics if you carry a dedicated GPS device. Just like a phone, they can break, not have reliable satellite connections, or the batteries can die. **Always have a map and compass as a backup.**

Maps, compasses and GPS apps and devices all have specific vocabularies to learn. At first all these terms can be confusing, but with a bit of practice you can learn what each term means and how it applies to finding your way in the wilderness.

Wilderness navigation is like any other outdoor skill. You can learn the basics by studying books, YouTube courses, or taking a class and then practicing close to home. You can become an expert in outdoor navigation if you enjoy the process. As you gain competence in these skills you will also gain confidence in your ability to find your way where you want to go and get back home again. This confidence will make your outdoor adventures with your family more relaxed and enjoyable. Start small with trails that are well marked. Then you can challenge yourself with longer distances and more remote trails. Eventually you can even learn to travel through the backcountry without a trail. It is a good feeling to know you can always find your way to a specific destination in the wilderness and then get back home again.

**Checklist of navigation principles –**
- ✓ We have learned basic map and compass skills.
- ✓ We are developing our direction finding skills.
- ✓ We know how to use the tools we have chosen.
- ✓ We are starting small on well-marked trails.
- ✓ We keep the mindset that we will always find our way in the backcountry.

# Chapter 14
## Put This in Your Pack
### the gear you need and nothing more

**Tips -**
- Develop an essentials kit system
- Use one of the suggested checklists to create your own system
- Learn to use each part of your essentials system
- Let kids develop their own age appropriate essentials kits

The living room is cluttered from one end to the other with backpacking gear. Three packs are slumped against the wall waiting to receive all the gear we'll carry for the next 4 days. This is the usual chaos before every backpacking trip.

"Do you have the kits checklists?"

"Yeah, right here."

My daughter holds up a clipboard with printed copies of our checklists clamped into it.

"OK, Let's start with the essentials."

"I'll go over the food kits while you guys do the gear."

My friend sorts through the zip bags piled on the kitchen table making separate piles for each of us. We check each kit and make sure we're not missing anything. Then, one by one, the kits get packed into the backpacks.

"You're starting to look a bit lopsided there honey."

My daughter's pack tilts to the left ominously. She swaps some gear around and soon it stands straight.

"Is that everything?"

She checks over the lists one more time.

"Wait, did you get toilet paper?"

I shuffle through the side pocket of my pack.

"Yep, I do. Do you?"

"Yes."

My friend checks her toilet kit.

"I've got mine too. Did you check each of the dog packs?"

We're each taking our dogs along and the dogs carry their own gear, except my daughter's little dog. He gets out of that duty.

"All here. I'll fill up the water bottles and then make sure they're balanced and we'll be good to go."

Forty five minutes later our formerly slumped packs are now standing at attention against the wall, straps snugged up tight and ready to load into the car.

"OK! Time for the test!"

I hold up a luggage scale. It's time to weigh our packs and see if we're within our limits of 35 lbs max with food and water. We hang each pack on the scale (including the dog packs). 28 lbs (my daughters), 30 lbs (mine), 32 lbs (my friends).

"Close enough. Let's call it good. We'll load up in the morning and hit the road early."

Over many years of planning trips and organizing gear, I've found a system that works for me. Rarely do we forget any important gear and the packing process goes smoothly most of the time. In the early years I spent days gathering gear, making lists, checking and rechecking packs. The thought of forgetting some important piece of equipment kept me up at night. After all, my little ones were depending on me to be prepared! After a few trips with missing pieces of gear, I discovered we always were just fine. We adapted, improvised, and ended up comfortable and safe in spite of a missing pot or tent stakes. I still like to be prepared but I'm much more relaxed about making sure we have everything. I have the experience and skills to make do with what nature provides. Sometimes I take minimalist trips and intentionally "forget" to bring important gear just to challenge myself. Those are trips I take alone or with other experienced backpackers but I enjoy testing my skills.

When you start out backpacking with your kids there are some basic things you need to be safe and comfortable. These few things don't need to be expensive or top of the line. They don't have to be name brand or ultralight. They don't even have to belong to you. Borrowing gear is a great way to get started. In this chapter I will describe some basic "kits" you can put together to make packing easier and make sure your needs are covered. The best gear can serve more than one use. This saves weight and space in your pack. A bandana can be used for a handkerchief, an arm sling, a compress, a hat, a sunshade for your neck, a washcloth, a towel, a hot pad, and a face mask around a smoky fire. Most gear won't be able to cover this many uses, but think of as many applications for a piece of gear as you can. The exception to this rule is for fire starters and certain tools. In some survival gear you want redundancy. You need at least 3 ways to light a fire. Tools such as knives and lights should have a backup plus a way to sharpen the blades and extra batteries for the lights. The more essential to survival a piece of gear is, the more likely you'll want some kind of backup. We'll discuss this in more detail.

**The Essentials**
There are several schools of thought when it comes to emergency essentials to carry with you into the

backcountry. All of these essential kit lists are sufficient for backpackers. You can consider the two I describe here or do some research and come up with your own plan. Just be sure every adult or teen has these essentials with them at all times. I've listed "Kid Kits" in Appendix A that can grow with your kids. Each kid should carry an essentials kit with them at all times. Carry a fanny pack or day pack even when you are away from camp so you are never without these essentials.

The most traditional list among backpackers is known as "The Ten Essentials". "The Ten Essentials" is a list of 10 items (or groups of items) that you should always have with you when you venture into the wilderness. The first "Ten Essentials" list was compiled in the 1930's by The Mountaineers, a Seattle-based organization for climbers and outdoor adventurers. The idea behind the list was to help people be prepared for emergencies they may face while exploring the outdoors. The list was changed in 2003 to a group of systems rather than individual items.

Theoretically, with proper knowledge and skill, you can survive with just these 10 items in your pack or pockets if you get injured or stranded unexpectedly and can't make it back to your car or to get help. These are essential items you need with you on any hike that takes you away from your car or civilization. On most hikes you won't use most of these things, but when you really need them, they can save your life. It is important to know how to use each of these 10 items.

## Updated Ten Essential "Systems"
1. Navigation (map and compass)
2. Sun protection (sunglasses and sunscreen)
3. Insulation (extra clothing)
4. Illumination (headlamp/flashlight)
5. First-aid supplies
6. Fire (waterproof matches/lighter/candles)
7. Repair kit and tools
8. Nutrition (extra food)
9. Hydration (extra water)
10. Emergency shelter

**The Ten C's**

There are several other schools of thought in the outdoor survival community. Many outdoor survival schools develop kits and lists they think best cover a person in a wilderness survival situation. These all have their merits and any one of them would meet your needs for survival. My favorite was created by Dave Canterbury at Self Reliance Outfitters. The concept includes The Ten C's" of survival. Each "C" stands for a part of your gear that you need to be safe in the wilderness. I find it helpful for remembering the important areas of gear.

The "Ten C's" are the essential pieces of gear you should always have with you. Much like the "Ten Essentials", this gear will cover all your basic needs in the wilderness. You and your family can readily survive with just ultralight versions of these 10 pieces of gear. The full set of Ten C's includes everything you need to backpack comfortably. There are many different ways you can create your Ten C's kits. A full set of backpacking gear for you and your family should include all of the Ten C's. I use this concept for all my outdoor adventures, whether day hikes to several day trips. Find a checklist online to work from.

*Cutting Tool*
I've taken many backpack trips with a simple Swiss Army knife tucked into my pack or pocket. For most backpacking needs it is sufficient. It's a tool for cutting cheese or cordage. It's lightweight and easy to carry. There are hundreds of variations on the Swiss Army knife theme and many good ones. Take some time at your local hardware or outdoor store and you'll discover the variety of choices available.

I have found that, while I will always include a small pocket knife in my backpacking gear, I am not satisfied to carry only one small knife any more. In a real emergency situation, when your cutting tool is needed for building a shelter, making feather sticks for building a fire in the rain, and even "batoning" (chopping) wood to keep your fire going, a small knife isn't sufficient for the tasks. I now also carry a larger fixed blade knife that I know can hold up under the strain of a true emergency situation. You don't need a 10" Rambo blade for your larger knife. A solid full-tang (the blade metal goes all the way to the end of the handle) blade about 4" long with a flattened back (the part that isn't sharpened) is sufficient. The best blades for survival are made of carbon steel so they can help you start a fire with your Ferro rod (more about that in a minute). Most of these knives weigh about 5 oz. You'll need a good lightweight sheath to protect the sharp blade from damage and from cutting you and your gear.

*Combustion*
You should always have at least three different tools for starting a fire with you. Fire IS the factor that can save you

and your children's lives in an emergency situation. Learning to build a fire takes practice... lots of practice. It looks easy on You Tube videos and it may even be easy in the backyard on a sunny day with wood that's been drying for two years. In the wilderness, and always in emergency situations, you won't find conditions so favorable. Usually when you need a fire the most, it is wet, snowy, cold and the burnable dead wood around you in the forest is saturated with water.

There are many tricks to finding the best wood possible. Always use dead wood. It doesn't do any good to chop down a living tree to make a fire. The wood is green and won't burn well (or at all) and it destroys a living tree unnecessarily. Look for dead wood that is off the ground. Dead limbs on live trees. Small dead trees that are still standing. Remember, we are talking about survival situations. Always follow regulations for fires when you are backpacking. But build a fire when you and your children's lives depend on it. Fires provide heat to keep core body temperatures at safe levels and they can be used to signal your location.

Combustion tools include lighters, Ferro cerium rod, waterproof fire starters, waterproof/windproof matches, and emergency candles. The three that I carry with me are a medium to large sized Ferro rod, a mini Bic lighter, and waterproof fire starter that I make at home. Most of the time redundancy in gear will just add weight to your pack, but emergency tools should always have a backup. I carry a lighter in my kitchen kit for lighting the stove. I carry a lighter in my essentials kit that goes with me everywhere. I carry a ferro rod in my essentials kit and several waterproof fire starters. Don't skimp on your ferro rod. A tiny rod can break or get used up rather quickly. It's better to carry a medium to large size. Waterproof fire starters are made up of a combustible material (such as an egg carton or cotton ball) saturated in a waterproof burnable material (such as wax or petroleum jelly). There are many commercial brands of waterproof fire starter. Check out your local outdoor store or do some research and make your own. It's a simple project your kids will love.

Learn how to make sparks with your Ferro rod onto your fire starter to get a small flame going. You'll need a striker to strike sparks off of the rod. I have used cut up pieces of hacksaw blade or metal strikers that sometimes come with a Ferro rod. If you have a fixed blade knife made of carbon steel and a squared off top (the part of the knife that isn't sharpened) then you can throw a lot of sparks from your Ferro rod with the back of your knife. It's a skill you must develop just like starting a fire in the rain. A Ferro rod is the most dependable of these fire starting tools. It still sparks if it gets wet, unlike matches (even waterproof matches). It isn't affected by cold or elevation like a lighter. And a larger rod withstands a lot of abuse.

Combustion includes food, the fuel for you and your children's bodies. I covered food lists in Chapter 6. Don't forget to carry emergency food when you are on day hikes.

*Cover*
Cover includes all the things you will need to shelter yourself in the backcountry. Not just your tarp or tent but your clothing, shoes, a hat, sunscreen, and sunglasses. Ask yourself what you need to protect yourself and your children from the elements and choose lightweight options to cover your needs.

When you are backpacking, you will have your tarp or tent in your pack. But if you leave camp for a day hike you still need to have cover with you. Cover can be as simple as a garbage bag or a survival blanket. A poncho can double as rain gear as well as a shelter. An extra lightweight tarp is easy to carry and set up and more weather resistant for a group that includes children. You can also carry cheap and lightweight painter's drop cloths to make emergency shelter. They will probably only last one use but that is all you will need it for. A shiny or bright colored cover can double as a signaling device. Having these lightweight backup shelters takes care of the redundancy you need in essential gear.

*Container*
The pack you carry your gear in is your main container. A pack is one of the "Big 3" gear items that make up the core of your outdoor kit. Packs come in many sizes, weights, and designs. You need a pack large enough to carry what you need but not so large that you'll unconsciously fill it up with more than you need. A pack about 40L (or 3000 CI) is a good size. Finding a pack that fits well and is lightweight takes some research and some testing but is well worth the effort.

Your cookpot, water bottle, and dishes for eating are other containers you will need. The best cook pots have a snug lid and a bail for hanging over a fire. Side handles are handy too but not essential. Choose a cookpot big enough to cook food for your entire group. Small cook pots are wonderful for solo hikes but are frustrating when cooking for a group. As mentioned in Chapter 6, aluminum pots are cheap and lightweight and an inexpensive way to get started in backpacking. Stainless steel pots are tough and affordable and will get handed down to your kids when you retire from backpacking. Titanium is nearly indestructible and very lightweight but costs significantly more. Don't be afraid of used cooking gear. It will give you an inexpensive way to learn your preferences for your cook pots.

Even on a day hike you should carry some kind of metal container you can use over a fire. A simple solution is to carry a stainless steel or titanium water bottle. This serves double duty as your water bottle and can also be used to boil water if you don't make it back to your camp or your car before dark. Be sure to remove any plastic lids before putting on the fire! There are Sierra mugs that hook onto a pack easily and are lightweight. You can also carry one of your smaller camp pots when you leave camp. It is important to stay hydrated and a metal container will allow you to boil water for purification and for warm drinks even if you are stranded away from your camp. Pack a few bags of tea and some pemmican and you are set for an emergency overnighter.

*Cordage*
Cordage has many essential uses for camp and emergencies alike. Cordage will simplify shelter building both in camp and for emergency shelters. It can help mend broken pack straps and even make a carrying device. It can be used for splints in first aid and many other applications. You will need cordage for hanging bear bags and gear safely in trees.

550 Para cord is one of the most familiar outdoor cordages and is widely available. It is a rope made of a nylon sheath with 7 2-ply yarns that make up the center. The rope can be cut and the inner yarns removed and used for small tasks such as fishing line and sewing. The outer mantle is still

usable even if the inner yarns are removed. 550 Para cord was originally designed for the suspension lines of parachutes but has proved extremely useful for a variety of situations both military and civilian. 100 yards of 550 Para cord is a good amount to carry.

If 100 yards of 550 is too bulky, you can carry a smaller amount and make up the yardage difference with bankline. Bankline is a tar impregnated nylon twine with many uses. It creates knots that hold very well. It is waterproof and can be used for just about any tying job you can think of. It is also an alternate waterproof fire starter. Ultra lightweight cordage comes in many brands and styles. It can save significant weight but is expensive. Even 100 yards of cheap nylon rope from your hardware store will suffice for cordage. Don't forget to include it in your essentials gear.

*Candle*
A source of light is more than a convenience in the outdoors. When all goes well, a simple mini squeeze light is sufficient for most needs. When conditions become challenging, a brighter source of light is needed. It is wise to have 2 sources of light. This doesn't have to be elaborate or expensive. A tiny squeeze light weighs a couple of ounces and costs very little. Pair that with a decent headlamp and you will have all your lighting redundancy needs covered.

Headlamps rule the night for backpackers. They allow you to work hands free and can be directed to illuminate just the area you need lit up. Headlamps are available in a wide variety of brightness, energy efficiency, weights, and prices. Choose an inexpensive headlamp to begin and upgrade to a brighter more dependable one when you start taking longer trips.

Included in this C is candles. Emergency candles have multiple uses. They can provide soft lighting, help with fire starting, and even lubricate a squeaky piece of gear.

*Compass*
A reliable compass and a good topographical map are essential parts of your kits when you head into the backcountry. Of course these are of little use if you don't learn to use them. You don't have to be an expert with a map and compass but you do need to understand and practice the basics to find your way in the wilderness. One of the advantages of a compass and map is how lightweight they are to carry. These are tried and true tools that won't let you down. Chapter 13 covers how to use map, compass and GPS in detail.

A GPS is a handy tool to have. Many backpackers use GPS apps on their smartphone and take a charging device to keep their phone powered. A GPS device or app can give you very accurate information about where you are, how far you've traveled, and how far you have left to go. As convenient as GPS devices are, they are far more likely to fail than a compass and map. Batteries run out. The sun doesn't shine to charge your phone with your solar charger. Your device gets lost or ruined. If you carry a GPS, don't neglect your map and compass skills or fail to carry a compass and map with you at all times.

*Cargo Tape*
Also known as duct tape, cargo tape has as many uses as a bandana! Pack and clothing repairs are covered with a compact roll of quality cargo tape. Cuts can be sealed up, bandages affixed, and injuries supported. Tarp repairs, shoe

repairs, and makeshift gear are all possible with a bit of cargo tape in your pack.

*Canvas Needle*
I sometimes combine cargo tape and canvas needle into a repair kit that covers many possible problems in the wilderness. A canvas needle, also called a sail needle, is a sturdy needle with a very sharp point. Besides the obvious sewing repairs, a canvas needle can serve as a makeshift compass, help remove a splinter, drain fluid from a blister, and other delicate operations. The threads inside 550 Para cord can be used with a canvas needle. I also like to carry a small container of dental floss for sewing on buttons and flossing teeth.

Gear lists abound online and in backpacking books. It can be overwhelming to see how many choices are available for each piece of gear. Don't despair! If you focus on each of these 10 C's and find gear you can afford that fits each category, you will be covered. There are hundreds of different combinations of gear that will meet your needs. There isn't a wrong way to do this so go ahead and dive in. You will eventually create your own system that works for you and your family.

## Conclusion
Take everything you need to be safe and comfortable when you are backpacking. But remember that part of being safe and comfortable is not carrying more than your body can handle. This is an ever evolving discipline that becomes part of your outdoor adventures. Each trip you take is another step in developing your perfect balance between comfort and pack weight.

**Checklist -**
- ✓ We have chosen an essentials system.
- ✓ We know how to use each part of our system.
- ✓ Each family member carries age appropriate essentials.
- ✓ We are flexible to try new tools and learn to use them.

See Appendix A for kid-friendly and age appropriate safety kits you can build with your kids.

## Chapter 15
## Bears Live Here
### How to keep kids safe in the wild

**Tips**
- know the dangers and risks of taking kids into the wilds
- don't let fear stop you from exploring the outdoors or from having fun
- don't anthropomorphize wildlife– learn the true nature of animals and respect them
- be calm and don't panic
- prepare yourself and your kids to meet the challenges

We started our trip around the Three Sisters Mountains on a sunny day in August. Our group of 10 were heading out on a 5 day hike. About 2 miles into our hike, the summer skies opened up and fell on us in the form of heavy rain. Thunder and lightning raged around us. Within minutes the trail became a small river. We attempted to get off the trail and take shelter under trees and bushes, but soon realized the storm wasn't going to stop and we were going to have to finish our 4 mile hike to Green Lakes in the deluge. We trudged on in ankle deep water, soaked from head to toe. The storm abated by the time we reached our campsite and we were able to set up our tarps and tents in dry conditions. We started a fire and did our best to dry our boots and gear.

The next day was clear and beautiful as is usual in summer in Central Oregon. We had managed to dry most of our gear except for our boots. Our destination was 7 miles away and we started early. At a trail junction we all took a wrong turn.

We corrected our error and got back on track in plenty of time to reach camp before dark. But our 7 mile hike turned into a 14 mile hike by the time the day was done. This would have presented a challenge under normal circumstances but hiking in wet boots caused every one of us to get severe blisters. Even those of us who rarely suffered from them. We finished our 43 mile hike without further incident, but in far more discomfort that we would have liked. Looking back on it, we would have been better off to take a day and rest, recover, get our boots fully dry before attempting to hike those 7 (turned 14) miles. Today, I would have encouraged everyone to hike in sandals and keep their boots dry to avoid the problem all together. Each trip I take into the wilderness is another step in gaining experience in handling unforeseen situations.

Unexpected weather and trail conditions are a fact of backpacking. As adults, we can choose to accept the discomfort and trudge on and stay on our planned schedule. But when hiking with kids you don't always have the option to push through

Family adventures in the outdoors are exciting ways to build memories with your kids. But the nature of the raw wilderness opens the possibilities of dangers and hazards that need to be thoughtfully considered. I have found that being educated and prepared are the best preventions to keep challenging situations from turning tragic.

Below I've listed possible hazards you may face in the wild and how to prevent problems. Although this is not a comprehensive list, it covers the most likely scenarios you will find in the wilderness. The above story is probably the worst situation you and your family will face in the outdoors. But a little knowledge will help you avoid any truly serious problems while backpacking.

Before you get overwhelmed with the potential dangers and lock yourself and kids up at home, remember that statistically, driving to the grocery store is potentially more deadly than any of the below hazards combined. **Use common sense and don't let fear stop you from spending time in the outdoors and sharing your passion with your kids.**

**Weather**
*Thunderstorms*
Summer thunderstorms are common in some places and a thunderstorm in the mountains, especially above tree line, has its own set of dangers. Thunderstorms occur more often in the afternoon in mountainous regions. If you know there are thunderstorms forecasted for the area you are hiking, plan to be off high peaks and ridges by noon. Lightening usually strikes the highest standing objects in an open area. If you are above the tree line you are often the highest standing object. When you see or hear a thunderstorm approaching be calm, but get to a safe area quickly. Even if you hear thunder approaching and don't see lightning, you are still at risk. Look for a group of small trees surrounded by larger trees and shelter in the center of the smaller trees. You can also shelter in a dry, low area like a small ravine. Avoid damp ground or open areas, lone and tall trees and rocky outcroppings and ledges. If you are forced to shelter in the open, find the driest and lowest place you can – a shallow ditch or depression that doesn't have water in it or a

dry valley. Then make yourself a small target. Squat with your heels touching and your head between your knees and cover your ears. Have your children take the same position and squat together but not touching each other. Be sure you remove your packs and anything you are carrying that will stand tall and pointed. Such as fishing poles, tent poles, or hiking poles. Do not shelter in a tent out in the open or anywhere in or around bodies of water.

Thunderstorms frequently bring heavy rain. Stay away from ravines and areas that show evidence of high levels of water even if they are dry. These fill quickly with water in flash floods and are extremely hazardous. Be conscience of steep hillsides where heavy rain water rushes down, bringing rocks and debris with it. Mud and rock slides happen quickly and unexpectedly. When soils become saturated with water, steep slopes are vulnerable to these slides. Pay attention when hiking on trails with steep slopes above or below you in heavy rains.

In heavy rains, small creeks and rivers can quickly become impassible. This is especially true when creeks and rivers originate in glaciers high on mountains. The heavy rains cause snow and ice melt that causes creeks and rivers to rise rapidly. Even if the rain and thunderstorm is not directly over your location, it can still cause rapid water rise in these glacier-fed creeks and streams if it is raining higher in the mountains.

Most summer thunderstorms are short lived and add spectacular excitement to being in the outdoors up close and personal. But take precautions and keep you and your family safe.

*Windstorms*
Strong winds can blow in quickly in mountainous areas. Check the weather forecast before you leave on your trip and learn to be a sky-watcher when you are outdoors. Simply paying attention to your surroundings and watching the weather patterns can significantly reduce your risk of being caught off guard. When a windstorm blows in, find shelter among strongly rooted trees. As discussed in the chapter on setting up camp, look above you and around for dead trees and branches that could fall on your shelter area. Get below ridges and high peaks. Try to find an area the wind is not affecting as severely. This might be behind a ridge or a rise in the ground. If you are in an area with few trees, blowing dirt and sand could become hazardous. Look for areas of calm. Even small groups of bushes or small hills can make the difference between miserable and comfortable. Take enough time to choose wisely when seeking shelter.

*Cold and Wet Conditions*
When cold rains settle in, living and traveling in the wilderness can be unpleasant. If you are not paying attention to your own physical well-being or that of your children then cold, rainy weather can become dangerous.

Hypothermia is a condition of the body having a lower than normal body temperature. This can range from a few degrees too low to dangerously low. The conditions that most commonly cause hypothermia are often relatively mild. Perhaps it is the seemingly low risk weather that causes hikers to not notice that they're becoming too cold. Wet clothing causes the body to lose heat. When hiking and generating body heat you may not notice that you are becoming colder than is safe. Children, in particular, lack the awareness to adequately care for their needs. If you are hiking in these conditions, try to stay dry if you can. Often this isn't realistic. If you or your kids are wet from rain and staying wet, feel their hands and feet frequently to monitor their body temperature. Look for color changes around their mouths (whiter or bluer than usual). As soon as you can, set up camp and strip off wet clothes. Take the time to boil water and give hot drinks to everyone in your group. Share body heat to warm little bodies (or adult bodies if needed) and keep your insulated gear as dry as possible.

Do not hesitate to build a fire to keep you and your family from getting dangerously cold and wet if the conditions warrant it. No matter the fire bans in place, your priority and responsibility is first to care for the safety of your family. Perfect your fire making skills so you know you can start and safely maintain a fire in the pouring rain or sleeting snow.

*Unexpected Snowstorms*
Snowstorms can happen any time of year at high elevations. Check the weather forecast before venturing into the mountains and be prepared for the worst conditions. It isn't reasonable to carry full winter gear on a summer outing, but make sure you have clothing that can keep you dry and insulated. You can create insulation in an emergency with your sleeping bags and sleeping pads as well as with natural materials such as fir boughs, dead leaves, and dead grasses. Know the signs of hypothermia and watch each member of your group carefully. Children can become hypothermic quickly. If your child is unusually difficult, inconsolable, or

lethargic, get them warm and dry as quickly as possible. Put them inside a sleeping bag with you and give them warm drinks if they are conscious and able to drink.

I reiterate my encouragement to start a fire to keep you and your family safe from unexpected cold. This is easier said than done, and I strongly encourage you to perfect your fire building skills and be confident you can build a fire in any and all weather conditions.

Other hazards of unexpected snowstorms include low visibility for traveling and significant changes to the way the environment looks. Trail signs may be covered or knocked down. Hills and valleys once familiar to you can suddenly look all the same. In summer snowstorms, it is often best to find a safe place to shelter and stay put until the storm passes and the snow melts off a bit before trying to travel.

As in all wilderness situations, stay calm and don't panic. Panic causes more tragedies than any other condition in the wilds. You will see your way through the difficult situation if you stop and think.

*Heat and Sun Exposure*
There are three heat related syndromes to be aware of when you are exposed to sun and high heat. They are listed from least dangerous to most dangerous below.

The first is heat cramps, which is cramps in the muscles that occur during and after exercise. Legs are the most commonly affected areas but you can get abdominal cramps as well. Muscles cramp or spasm while exercising and the body is sweating heavily. Fatigue, nausea, and vomiting can also be part of heat cramps. Preventions for heat cramps are staying hydrated with plenty of water and electrolyte drinks during and after exertion. If you get heat cramps, stop exercising, drink water, and massage the affected area. It is safe to resume exercise when the cramps are gone.

The second is heat exhaustion, caused by dehydration and a loss of electrolytes. When you are active and sweating a lot, it is important to replace fluids with water and electrolyte drinks. When you get dehydrated, your body can't sweat enough to cool itself sufficiently. Your body temperature rises and eventually leads to heat exhaustion. Symptoms include fatigue, headache, weakness, nausea, vomiting, and decreased coordination. It is possible to experience fainting, profuse sweating, normal to slightly elevated body temperature and sometimes a drop in blood pressure. Prevention includes drinking plenty of water and replacing electrolytes during heavy exercise. If you or your child show any signs of heat exhaustion, immediately find a cool place and rest. Drink water and electrolytes. If blood pressure drops, get emergency help as quickly as possible. If you do suffer from heat exhaustion it's best to rest for at least 24 hours and then avoid exercising in the heat for a week.

This is difficult to do if you suffer heat exhaustion while hiking in the backcountry and need to get home under your own power. Prevention is the very best policy. If you must hike out after experiencing heat exhaustion, hike in the cool hours of the day and keep a damp bandana on your neck. Keep your head covered with a hat and rest often.

The third syndrome is heat stroke, the most serious of the three syndromes. It can turn deadly very quickly. It occurs when the body fails to regulate its temperature and the body's temperature continues to rise. If left untreated, heat stroke can lead to seizures, stroke, and death. Heat stroke can happen even when a body is sweating profusely but the sweating fails to cool the body temperature. Symptoms include high body temperature (106 or higher), lack of sweating, red and dry skin, confusion and altered consciousness, convulsions, difficulty breathing, and a fast heart rate. Prevention begins with paying attention to body temperature in high heat situations and drinking water and electrolyte drinks. If symptoms begin, send for help immediately. Get the victim into a cool place, undress and expose their skin to cool air, and apply cool water and ice to groin, underarms, and neck until help arrives.

Stay aware of how you and your children are feeling when you are hiking in the heat. Be especially aware when you are tired and likely not to pay as close attention as usual. All heat related syndromes are preventable if you stay aware and stay hydrated.

**Wildlife**
One of the joys of hiking in the wilderness is getting the opportunity to observe wildlife in their natural habitats. If treated with the proper respect, wildlife hazards are not too difficult to manage. The greatest risk humans face with wildlife is not understanding their nature. Anthropomorphizing, or giving human attributes to animals, greatly increases your risks of being harmed by an animal you simply don't understand and that you expect to behave in ways it never will naturally. Avoid the extremes in attitudes toward wildlife. On one end of the spectrum is that these creatures are cuddly, safe animals that will act like a human or a domesticated pet. At the other end is the view

that wildlife is bloodthirsty and ready to attack at first sight. Neither of these attitudes about wildlife are accurate or helpful. It is worth your time to learn and teach your children the true nature of animals you may encounter on the trail. Watch documentaries and nature shows. Read books from authors who have studied animals up close. Visit wildlife sanctuaries to see up close what these animals look like, their relative size, and a glimpse into their habits. This is a great way to spend winter months together while anticipating hiking trips. Be wise in how much reality you expose your kids to in regard to wildlife. Consider their ages and abilities to reason. Your goal is to set realistic expectations and knowledge rather than fear and sensationalized views of animals. Find out the facts about the different wild animals you may encounter and educate yourself and your kids.

Become familiar with the area you are hiking in. Is it known for a large bear population? Which kinds of bears live there? Have cougars been sighted recently? Do your homework before setting out and learn the habits of the creatures whose territories you are visiting. In my experience, I see far less wildlife when hiking with a noisy bunch of kids than when I am alone. But you do need to know the ways that children are at greater risk for harm from some wildlife than adults and keep a close eye on your kids.

*Bears*
Many areas where humans hike are homes to bears. Know the type of bear you may encounter in the area you are hiking in. The most common in the lower 48 states in America is the black bear. In general, black bears are shy

creatures, and if you do get to see one, they are often running away from you. Black bears are very good tree climbers and will usually choose retreat if given the option. But if threatened, black bears tend to be more likely to follow through on threats than their larger cousins, brown bears.

Any mother bear with cubs will instinctively protect them from perceived threats. If you see bear cubs, remember they are not teddy bears. Stop and take stock of your surroundings. Gather your kids close to you and make noise. Stay in an open area and avoid heavy brush. When you can see your way clear, move out of the area cautiously, keeping your kids close.

Any bear will protect a recent kill or food territory. If you come across a dead animal that looks like it has been covered or an attempt to hide it has been made, know this is some creatures dinner stash and they will likely return to it. Stop, look around, and move out of the area quickly. Keep alert when hiking through areas rich in wild berries. These are favorite places for bears to hang out and feed. Make plenty of noise and do your best not to startle a bear. Bears also feed on insects and fish. Torn rotting logs are signs of bear activity. Streams and rivers with schools of fish running are places very likely to attract bears. Be very careful setting up camp near these areas that are attractive to bears.

On the trail — when hiking through bear country, make plenty of noise on the trail. Sing songs, talk, and even consider putting bells on children's feet. Bears will avoid human contact if possible, and making noise gives them the chance to flee before you come up on them unexpectedly.

Carry bear pepper spray and keep it handy. This is a deterrent when sprayed in the face of an attacking bear. Study the directions that come with the canister. You need to spray it correctly for it to be effective and to keep from spraying yourself in the face. Learn to avoid contact with bears. It is a much better option.

In camp — in areas with large populations of bears, cook your food 200 or more feet away from sleeping areas. Hang all food, toiletries, and strong smelling items in a tree. There are several ways to do this and the area you are camping in will determine which method is the best for you. Basically, a rope is slung up over a high branch and the food bag is raised until out of bear reach (15 feet or more). There are many downsides to hanging bear bags and it is much more difficult out on the trail than you might imagine. You have to find a tree with a branch you can throw a rope over. It has to be a strong branch. It has to be high enough off the ground to be out of reach of bears. And you have to be able to tie off the rope to something sturdy and strong.

If there are no trees, hang food off of a rock face or a bridge, or store it out of a bear's sight off the trail and downwind of camp. Don't forget where you stashed it! An alternative to hanging a bear bag is to carry a container that is bear proof. (See resources at the end of the chapter.) These are difficult to use when you are hiking with children because they limit the amount of food you can pack and they are quite heavy. However, they do have their advantages and some areas give you no choice and require this option. Bear proof containers can also be hung in a tree to double protect your food items.

If you come across a bear, stop and evaluate. According to the Alaska Department of Natural Resources you should "STAY CALM. Attacks are rare. Bears may approach or stand on their hind legs to get a better look at you. These are curious, not aggressive, bears. BE HUMAN. Stand tall, wave your arms, and speak in a loud and low voice. DO NOT RUN! Stand your ground or back away slowly and diagonally. If the bear follows, STOP. If a bear is charging almost all charges are "bluff charges". DO NOT RUN! Olympic sprinters cannot outrun a bear and running may trigger an instinctive reaction to "chase". Do not try to climb a tree unless it is literally right next to you and you can quickly get at least 30 feet up. STAND YOUR GROUND. Wave your arms and speak in a loud low voice. Many times charging bears have come within a few feet of a person and then veered off at the last second." (http://dnr.alaska.gov/parks/safety/bears.htm)

Black bears are shyer than brown bears and are more likely to run than approach humans. However, statistically they are more likely to continue an attack once it has begun.

If attacked by a black bear:
- spray pepper spray at its face
- fight back and keep fighting
- keep children behind you
- yell, hit back with fists, sticks, rocks
- DO NOT run or climb a tree

Brown bears are often considered more dangerous because they are not as easily scared off as black bears. They are statistically more likely to attack than a black bear. However, they are also statistically more likely to stop an attack once it has begun. They tend to be more curious than their smaller cousins and will sometimes lose interest even after attacking.

If attacked by a brown bear:
- spray pepper spray at its face
- if the attack continues, drop to the ground and curl into a fetal position
- place children curled against your stomach and wrap your arms and legs around them in the fetal position, protecting your neck and head with your hands and arms
- play dead even if the bear makes contact, sometimes they will give up and lose interest, but stay in the fetal position until you are sure the bear has left the area
- DO NOT run
- if the attack does not stop even when you have lain still for a long time then fight back with sticks, rocks, and anything else you can get your hands on

*Cougars*

Cougars roam the Western United States and Canada. These are large loner cats, which are elusive and mysterious. Seeing a cougar in the wild is a rare event and if you do see one, it is likely they have been following you for a while. However, cougar numbers are on the rise and venturing more often into areas populated by humans. Cougars rarely attack adults and, if they do, it is usually an adult alone. Part of their mystery is that we still don't know exactly why cougars attack when they do. If a cougar does attack, it is far more likely to attack kids and it is quite common for cougars to attack pets.

Learn to identify cougar tracks. If you find dead animals hanging in trees or on high ledges, this is the cougar's kitchen. Gather your kids and pets and get out of the area, keeping alert.

As with bears, make plenty of noise on the trail. Keep dogs on leashes and keep your kids in sight. If you see a cougar cub, do not approach. Look around carefully. If you see an adult cougar, gather pets and kids close and give the cougar a route to escape. Don't corner them or approach them. Keeping your kids close, back out of the area slowly, keeping your eye on the cat. Make yourself look large and like a potential threat rather than timid prey.

If attacked by a cougar:
- don't back down
- maintain eye contact, make lots of noise, bare your teeth
- get as large as possible
- keep children behind you
- fight back with sticks, rocks, fists, aiming at the cougars face and eyes
- DO NOT run or act timid

*Wolves and Coyotes*

Wolves are being introduced to many wild areas in the Western United States. Their populations are growing and they are able to cover vast areas of territory. Wolves tend to avoid human contact if they can, but they are attracted to scents of food and smaller prey. Pets and children are the most vulnerable to wolf attacks. Wolf numbers are far lower than bears or cougars and are the least likely wild predator you will encounter while backpacking.

If you see a wolf, look around for other wolves. They typically travel in packs. Gather children and pets close and face the wolf you can see. If your group has more than one adult or includes a responsible teen, have them keep watch for other wolves. Maintain eye contact and remain calm, backing away from the wolf. Keep your dog under control. The majority of wolf attacks involve dogs.

If attacked by a wolf:
- maintain eye contact but avoid staring them down, make lots of noise
- step toward the wolf, don't appear timid
- get as large as possible, band together in a group
- keep children behind you
- fight back with sticks, rocks, fists, pepper spray
- DO NOT run or act timid

Coyotes are rarely threats to humans. They tend to be curious creatures and are often human habituated and have little fear when spotted. They are unlikely to act aggressive toward humans but they will protect themselves and their pups if they feel threatened. Coyotes do see dogs as a threat and sometimes as prey. Keep dogs on leashes to avoid encounters. Do not approach a coyote or coyote pups. Give them plenty of space to get away. In the rare event that a coyote becomes aggressive toward you, respond the same as for a wolf. As with wolves, the majority of coyote attacks involve dogs.

*Deer, Elk and Moose*
Deer, elk, and moose are the most common Cervidae you will encounter while hiking. Most of these hooved animals will flee at the first sign of a human. Like any wild animal, they will protect their young and their territories if they feel

threatened. They have razor sharp hooves, are very fast, and males have racks of antlers they use to protect themselves. Be especially aware during the spring when cervidae are having their babies. Also be aware during the fall breeding season. Males become quite aggressive and unaware of their surroundings. They are not looking for a fight with humans but they may mistake you for an enemy in their blind aggression toward other males they are competing with for mates.

Deer are very common in the United States and are often human habituated. Deer in wild places are more likely to be shy and will flee if given the opportunity. If you find a tiny fawn curled up on the ground, back away and don't touch it. It isn't abandoned and it doesn't need human help. A doe will leave her fawn hidden while she feeds a short distance away. Most danger from deer comes from deer in areas of heavy human use where they have been fed. They get accustomed to getting treats from humans they encounter and can get aggressive in insisting on getting those treats. Never feed any wild animal. You are not helping them and are causing them great harm if you do.

Elk are a much larger cousin of deer. They usually travel in small to large herds and tend to be elusive. They avoid human contact as much as possible. Like deer, they will protect themselves and their young if they feel threatened. Also like deer, they can become human habituated. Elk calves usually stay at their mother's side and it is rare to find them alone. Give elk space and they are most likely to move away from you.

Moose are even larger than elk, up to 1600 pounds and the size of a horse. They are more aggressive than elk and deer.

They have eyes placed on the sides of their heads, like most prey animals. This causes them to have a large blind spot in front of them. This is perceived as bad eyesight and it does function that way, however their eyesight is just fine. Moose are very territorial and will sometimes try to force humans out of their territory. Sometimes they will leave if a human is in the area and sometimes not. This makes them unpredictable. If you spot a moose, stop and take stock of your surroundings. Look for calves in the area and don't get between them and their mother. Stay still and see what the moose decides to do. If it moves away, wait for it to get out of sight before moving. Then go in a different direction if you can. If not, then move ahead cautiously and be on the alert. Keep children close and do your best not to startle a moose. Moose, like other prey animals, are distance sensitive. Give them plenty of space (at least 50 yards) and they are more likely to move away from humans. Get too close and they may attack. Never corner a moose (or any wild creature), or advance in a threatening way.

If threatened by a moose:
- Run! and try to get behind a large object or climb a tree
- you cannot outrun them so try to get to safety as quickly as you can
- if they make contact, curl into a ball, hide under logs or bushes, protect your head and neck from hooves and antlers
- keep kids protected underneath you
- DO NOT stand your ground, back off as fast as you can

*Small Mammals*
There are a variety of small furry animals you may encounter on your backpacking trips. Forests and wild lands are full of raccoons, skunks, marmots, squirrels, chipmunks, and other small mammals specific to various regions of the US. If left alone, these creatures offer little threat. Any animal will defend itself and it's young if it feels threatened. Teach children to admire wildlife from a distance. Even though these animals are relatively small they can still inflict wounds and sometimes carry diseases. Good wilderness ethics also demand leaving creatures in peace when visiting their homes.

One of the greatest risks from small rodents is the damage they can cause to gear in camp. Keep your camp clean, and keep all food put away in zip bags. Leave pack pockets unzipped to discourage these creatures from chewing through pack fabric to investigate. Enjoy their presence and do your best not to leave food around for them.

*Snakes*
There are 160 species of snakes in the United States. Only 20 of these are venomous. The best technique for dealing with snakes is to learn to avoid them. These are very shy creatures that will not attack humans unless they feel threatened. Learn the types of venomous snakes you might encounter in the areas you will be hiking with your kids. Teach them how to avoid these snakes. Don't allow children to play with any kind of snakes. Besides being very stressful for the snake, bites from nonvenomous snakes can still cause infections.

If hiking in areas known to have venomous snakes, stay on trails. Avoid high grasses and brush. Wear long pants and boots. Make sure a place is free from snakes before sitting down, going to the bathroom, or letting children explore and play.

If bitten by a venomous snake:
- keep the victim absolutely still and calm, restrict movement
- send someone for help immediately
- keep bite area below heart level
- do not cover bite area
- allow bite area to bleed freely for 15 to 30 seconds before cleansing
- cleanse bite area
- do not suction area by mouth
- do not cut bite area
- monitor vital signs
- get victim to hospital for treatment

*Insect Bites*
Insects, including biting insects, are a reality of spending time in the wilderness. Most biting insects are annoying but not dangerous. You should still know how to protect yourself from bites as much as possible and how to treat bites when they do occur.

Mosquitoes are common inhabitants of all wildlands. They reproduce at rapid rates in the early summer and swarm warm-blooded creatures mercilessly in their pursuit of their reproduction process. There are many repellants available for hikers with varying levels of effectiveness. Be cautious when using strong repellants with the active ingredient diethyltoluamide. Especially with children. DEET is a common repellant with this chemical. Essential oils can be used effectively but also warrant caution. Using head nets, long sleeves and long pants will help avoid these pesky critters. Learn how to find camps that avoid mosquitoes. Campsites with a breeze blowing through them and that are not close to standing water, for example. Mosquitoes are worse at certain times of the year. You may want to avoid these seasonal infestations if you are hiking with small children. Often in late summer the feeding frenzy has abated and your time in the wild will be more enjoyable.

Ticks are biting insects that grab hold of warm-blooded creatures as they pass by brush and thick branches. Ticks first crawl on their host looking for a sheltered, warm place with blood vessels close the the surface of the skin. They then embed themselves head first in the skin and gorge on blood until their backends are swollen. Some types of ticks carry diseases and if you are bitten you should seek medical treatment. Lyme's disease is one of these diseases to be aware of as it can have a long lasting impact on health. As gross as these creatures are, they can be avoided with a little caution.

When hiking in areas infested with ticks, stay on the trail. Avoid hiking through tall grasses and thick underbrush. Wear long pants with the bottoms secured or tucked into boots. Wear long sleeves buttoned tight at the wrist. The most important prevention when hiking with small children is to perform a physical check on their bodies at the end of each day. Pay close attention to areas like under the arms, the groin, buttocks, base of neck and hairline. Remove any ticks you find immediately. If you check often you can avoid deeply embedded ticks. If they do become imbedded, remove carefully with tweezers. Don't break off the head, which can cause infection if left behind. Take the bite victim to the doctor to be tested for Lyme's disease and/or removal of tick if you can't get it off safely.

Spider bites happen in the wilds no more frequently than at home. In some ways, tarp and tent living allows spiders to escape humans where they may be trapped in a house. Most spider bites can be treated like a mosquito bite. Keep the area clean to avoid infection. If the bite is itchy, apply antihistamine creams or cold packs and keep it covered if children can't avoid scratching them.

Very few spiders in America cause a health threat to humans. Keep a close eye on the bite area to determine if the bite was caused by one of the two spiders whose bites are harmful. Watch for the wound becoming a growing ulcer that is blue or black. This may be a bite from a brown recluse spider. Seek medical treatment as soon as possible. Black widow spider bites can cause abdominal cramping, fever, nausea, and excessive sweating. Seek medical treatment immediately if these symptoms occur.

In rare cases a bite victim may have an allergic reaction. Look for hives, a rapid, weak pulse, difficulty swallowing, severe swelling, difficulty breathing. This is an anaphylactic shock reaction to a bite and needs immediate medical treatment. You can give antihistamine medications to slow down these reactions until you reach professional emergency help.

*Bee and Scorpion Stings*
Scorpion stings are relatively rare in the US. They are rarely deadly but can cause intense pain. Use caution when digging in areas where scorpions may hide. Under bark, dead leaves, logs, etc.

Bees, wasps, hornets, and yellow jackets are all flying insects that inflict a painful sting when they feel threatened. Do your best to avoid these insects when hiking. Don't wear bright, colorful clothing that a bee may mistake for a flower. Avoid strong smelling perfumes and lotions that may attract bees. Keep an eye open when eating strong smelling foods and put all garbage in sealed zip bags. Keep your campsite clean. Sweet drinks and foods attract bees. Protect children by not giving them sodas or sweet drinks and candy while camping and hiking. Do NOT swat or swipe at bees. Calmly move away from them and take preventative precautions. Treat bee and scorpion stings the same. Antihistamine medications can reduce swelling. Cold packs and antihistamine creams can help with pain and swelling at the sting site. Watch for signs of allergic reaction. If you know a member of your family is allergic to bee stings, carry an epi-pen and keep it close at hand. If you see symptoms of anaphylactic shock, seek medical treatment immediately.

Insects are native to the natural environments we are visiting and each plays an important role in the ecosystem. It is our job to learn to coexist with them as peacefully as we can. The danger from these creatures is minimal and rarely causes threat to human life. Avoidance and acceptance is your best method of defense against the annoyance and pain they can inflict.

### Environmental Hazards
Hazards from the environment require attention and vigilance on the part of adults taking children into the wilds.

Pay attention to areas with drop offs and cliffs. Keep children away from undercut banks along rivers and oceans. Snowbanks can be undercut as well. Rock climbing is a natural draw for children. Save this activity for trips when you include specialized climbing gear. Falling from even short heights can cause serious injury.

We covered unsafe drinking water in Chapter 9. The younger a child is the more at risk they are if infected with a waterborne illness. Know how to use and maintain your water filter properly and how to find the best water possible. Don't allow yourself to run out of water without knowing where your next dependable water source is. Dehydration is a real threat to safety in the backcountry.

Wildfires are common in the summer months when most of us enjoy hiking. Be sure to check with the local forest service office in the area you plan to hike before leaving on your trip. Seeing smoke while on your hike does not mean a fire is close at hand. Smoke from wildfires can travel many miles from the origin of the fire. But if you see fire and flame then you must hike out to the nearest road immediately. Fires move incredibly fast and it is unpredictable where they will travel.

Water crossings take serious planning when hiking with small children. This is a topic too detailed for this chapter. Do your research. Never let children cross streams unsupervised, unless they are step-across-puddle size. Know the safest methods for crossing streams with smaller people and don't take risks. I recommend against taking children on hikes that require serious river crossings unless there is an established bridge or you plan to use a boat.

## In Conclusion

I have hiked for many years in the backcountry with children and inexperienced adults, and so far I have never experienced significant danger. There have been situations that could have become dangerous if we had not responded correctly. If you take the time to learn some basic skills and use common sense, it is very possible for you to hike with your children many miles from civilization and trailheads and be perfectly safe. This chapter is meant to get you thinking about what your responsibility is to protect your children and to give you some ideas of knowledge you need to acquire.

The dangers of living around moving vehicles and dense populations of humans day after day are far greater than the dangers of the wilderness. Wild animals cause significantly less harm to humans than the pets we encounter every day. Insects are a reality no matter where you are, and the way to respond to them is the same if you are at home or in the wilds. There are no great mysteries to keeping you and your family safe while you are backpacking. Some basic planning, some common sense, and a willingness to take stock and take responsibility for yourself and your children is all that is needed. Emergency services are not quickly accessible and the expense of sending rescue teams into the wilderness is high. You can be a part of the solution in keeping your family safe without relying unduly on professionals. They are there when we really need them and they are highly trained. But it is our job to avoid needing them.

When you examine your responsibility to the safety of your family you may want to consider becoming an armed citizen if:

- You hike in areas that are particularly wild or inaccessible.
- You have multiple children in your group to protect.
- You know the areas you hike have high densities of moose, bears, or other predators.

Then you may want to consider arming yourself with appropriate weapons. I'm not suggesting you need to carry a soldier's weight in weapons to be safe in the wilderness. Nor am I suggesting that predators in the wild are hiding behind every tree and trail bend to attack. This simply isn't true. 99% of the time wildlife will leave humans alone. However, predators and large wildlife are not to be trifled with either. They have learned to survive in harsh environments and they aren't afraid to inflict harm to do so. This isn't personal toward humans. It's survival. Being armed and having the knowledge to defend your family, should the worst happen, is something for a parent to think through when considering your responsibility to protect and care for your children.

And finally, **educating yourself and your children is part of the fun of becoming a responsible backpacker.** In Appendix A, I have included lists to help direct your education process. I would consider these the absolute minimum of the skills to learn to become proficient as a backpacker. Children can readily learn these skills, and at surprisingly young ages. Don't hesitate to give them the opportunity. I have not given ages for these levels. You know your child best and you can best determine what skills and responsibilities they are ready for. Both you and your children will hike with more confidence and have more relaxed trips as you learn and implement these skills. Above all, start small and have fun!

You don't have to tackle multi-day trips covering many miles right away. Ease your way into this grand adventure of backpacking and build your expertise. This is a lifetime activity after all, and there is no hurry.

## Checklist

- ✓ Do we weigh the safety risks on our chosen hike and prepare for them?
- ✓ Are we teaching our kids how to be safe in the wilderness?
- ✓ Have we educated ourselves on how to live with the wildlife we will encounter?
- ✓ Are we equipping ourselves and our kids with safety kits and the skills to use them?

## Resources for bear canisters:

- o BearVault ([http://www.bearvault.com/](http://www.bearvault.com/))
- o Ursack® ([http://www.ursack.com/](http://www.ursack.com/))
- o Backpacker's Cache ([http://www.backpackerscache.com/](http://www.backpackerscache.com/))
- o Wild Ideas, Bearikade ([http://www.wild-ideas.net/](http://www.wild-ideas.net/))
- o Counter Assault® Bear Keg®([https://www.counterassault.com/product/bear-keg/](https://www.counterassault.com/product/bear-keg/))

# Appendix A
# Safety Kits and Skills
## Kid-friendly safety kits to build

Below is a list of safety kits and skills that are appropriate for kids. Take the time to teach kids the skills needed to use each kit effectively and safely. You will be amazed at the confidence they gain from knowing and practicing these skills and carrying the tools they need!

Each person in your group should carry an age appropriate safety kit. If a person requires medication, antihistamines, or an epi-pen then these should be included in their kit even if the child is young. This way the needed medication is with your child even if you are not. It would be prudent to include written instructions with the medication describing what your child needs in case you are separated from them.

**Kid Safety Kits**
Level 1 kid's kit:
- An opened Mylar emergency blanket stored in an easy to open zip bag
- A whistle attached to the child
- Water bottle
- A snack in a bag they can easily open themselves
- Stocking cap and an extra layer
- Small flashlight attached to child (strobe setting is preferred)
- Comfort object (small stuffed animal, blanky, etc.)

Level 1 skill set:
- How to use a Mylar blanket for cover and signaling
- How to use a whistle to signal for help

- How to turn the flashlight to strobe setting
- Phrase to memorize: **Hug a Tree, cover** with an emergency blanket to be seen and sheltered.

Level 2 kid's kit:
- All of level 1 plus–
- A headlamp
- Signal mirror
- A "Boo-Boo" first aid kit
- 1 bandana w/ safety pins (many uses, triangular bandage, washcloth, compress, etc.)
  (2) 2"x2" Gauze Pad
  (10) Band-Aid (6 large, 4 small)
  (2) Steri-strips
  (2) Povidone-Iodine Prep pads
  (2) Alcohol Prep pads
  (2) Triple Antibiotic
  (2) Sting Relief Pad
  (2) Burn gel
  (1) Moleskin (2"x4" strip)
  (2) Lip ointment
  (2) Antihistamine tabs
  (2) Electrolyte tabs

Level 2 skill set
- Level 1 plus–
- How to use a signal mirror to signal for help
- How to use a boo boo kit for minor wounds
- How to use a headlamp to signal for help
- Level 2 phrase to memorize: **If in doubt, wait it out!**


Level 3 kid's kit

- All of level 1 and 2 plus—
- Small metal cup/pot
- Knife
- Fire starter kit
- Cordage
- Trauma first aid kit
    1 – Space blanket, to wrap up the patient and discourage shock
    6 – 4x4-inch non-stick gauze pads
    1 – 8x10-inch trauma pad
    1 – 4-inch Israeli dressing
    2 – Pairs of non-latex gloves
    1 – Roll of 1-inch tape
    1 – Ace bandage, self-adherent, 3 inches x 5 yards (replace this every year)
    1 – QuikClot ACS (clotting sponge)
    20 – Antiseptic wipes
    2 – Ammonia inhalant swabs (to revive the patient)
    1 each – CPR mask, tweezers, EMT shears, eyewash, burn gel packet
    1 each – Eye pad, tourniquet, triangle bandage, tube of Neosporin

Level 3 skill set:
- Levels 1 and 2 plus—
- How to locate and collect safe drinking water
- How to boil water to treat it
- Knife safety
- How to make feather sticks
- How to find good fire materials
- How to start and maintain a safe warming and cooking fire
- How to safely build a signal fire

- How to build a simple shelter with cordage, emergency blanket, and a knife
- How to use a trauma first aid kit

Level 3 phrase to memorize: **Water first, Shelter second, Food last**

Made in the USA
Monee, IL
13 October 2020